Series / Number 07-023

RESEARCH
DESIGNS

PAUL E. SPECTOR

Florida Mental Health Institute
Tampa, Florida

 SAGE PUBLICATIONS / Beverly Hills / London

For information address:

SAGE Publications, Inc.
275 South Beverly Drive
Beverly Hills, California 90212

SAGE Publications Ltd
28 Banner Street
London EC1Y 8QE, England

International Standard Book Number 0-8039-1709-0

Library of Congress Catalog Card No. L.C. 81-40888

FIRST PRINTING

When citing a professional paper, please use the proper form. Remember to cite the
correct Sage University Paper series title and include the paper number. One of the
two following formats can be adapted (depending on the style manual used):

(1) IVERSEN, GUDMUND R. and NORPOTH, HELMUT (1976) "Analysis of
Variance." Sage University Paper series on Quantitative Applications in the Social
Sciences, 07-001. Beverly Hills and London: Sage Pubns.

OR

(2) Iversen, Gudmund R. and Norpoth, Helmut. 1976. *Analysis of Variance.* Sage
University Paper series on Quantitative Applications in the Social Sciences, series
no. 07-001. Beverly Hills and London: Sage Publications.

CONTENTS

Editor's Introduction   5

1.0 Introduction   7

2.0 Basic Concepts   11

3.0 Basic Logic of Design   19

4.0 One-Group Designs   28

5.0 Multiple-Group Designs   39

6.0 Factorial Designs   54

7.0 Concluding Remarks   77

References   78

Editor's Introduction

RESEARCH DESIGN by Paul E. Spector is an introduction to the basic principles of experimental and nonexperimental design in the social sciences. Dr. Spector introduces the material slowly and gradually, beginning with the basic concepts of research design. He discusses the meaning of such elementary concepts as variables, control randomization, and confounding variables, to mention just a few examples. As in any good pedagogic introduction to a topic in research methodology, Dr. Spector takes nothing for granted and addresses the broadest possible audience.

After introducing the basic concepts necessary to an understanding of research design, Dr. Spector discusses the basic logic of research design, contrasting and comparing experimental and nonexperimental designs and research strategies. He provides ample coverage of threats to internal and external validity, including the problems of history, instrument reactivity, unreliability and invalidity, subject loss, Hawthorne effects, and others. The major nonexperimental, single-group designs are discussed, including pretest-posttest design; interrupted time series; and correlational designs, both cross-sectional and longitudinal. He provides several social science examples of these designs, including a study designed to assess the impact of reorganization in a Veterans Administration outpatient clinic on patient dropout, length of waiting lists, and time periods between appointments; a study designed to determine whether no-fault divorce laws tend to increase the number of divorces; and a study designed to test a theory relating suicide to the threat of war. In all of his examples, Dr. Spector is particularly sensitive to the limitations of each design, of caveats which must be added to any substantive conclusions that the researcher draws.

Dr. Spector gives most of his attention to the more complicated designs, most of which are experimental rather than nonexperimental, including multiple-group designs such as two-group designs; multiple-group posttest designs; multiple-group pretest-posttest designs; ex post facto designs; and multiple-group time series designs. His examples of these designs include a study to determine the impact, if any, of an experimental prison work release program; a study to determine the effects of job previews on job acceptance and survival of applicants to a telephone company; and a study to determine whether different operant conditioning procedures would be effective in reducing employee absenteeism in a hospital.

The final chapter of RESEARCH DESIGN is devoted to factorial designs, including two × two designs; Solomon four-group designs; M × N factorial designs; higher order factorial designs; hierarchical or nested designs; and designs with concomitant variables. Dr. Spector is particularly lucid in explaining factorial designs and nested designs, with a clear and concise examination of statistical interaction in factorial designs. His examples include a study to investigate the interactive effects on intrinsic motivation of initial task interest and goal setting and a study to sort out the impact of course content, instructor expressiveness, and instructor reputation on student evaluations of faculty. The examples that Dr. Spector draws on to illustrate the various designs he presents are from a wide range of social science disciplines and are, without exception, inherently interesting. Methodology pedagogues will be especially interested in his presentation of the research which examines the determinants of student evaluations of instructors.

Although it stands on its own, RESEARCH DESIGN is best read with the earlier paper in this series, ANALYSIS OF VARIANCE by Iversen and Norpoth. Dr. Spector makes ample reference to the statistical methods most appropriate to the analysis of data collected using various of these research designs, but his treatment is of the principles of design, not of analysis. This paper is best understood by those with familiarity with the analysis of variance.

— John L. Sullivan, Series Editor

1.0 INTRODUCTION

Any scientific investigation, be it in the social or natural sciences, must begin with some structure or plan. This structure defines the number and type of entities or *variables* to be studied and their relationship to one another. Such a structure is termed a design, the topic of this monograph, which will be limited to two varieties — experimental and nonexperimental.

A scientific investigation or study in the social sciences is undertaken to answer some specific question or hypothesis concerning the behavior of animals, humans, or social systems. Such questions may concern whether certain conditions, events, or situations cause particular behaviors or events or if certain conditions, events, situations, and behaviors occur together in time. For example, a social scientist might ask if unemployment causes crime, if inflation affects voter turnout for presidential elections, or if college students learn better with lecture or seminar course formats. Such questions lend themselves quite well to being answered with methods of scientific inquiry based on principles to be discussed in this monograph.

Of course it is not necessary to use scientific methods to answer questions. One might rely on intuition or educated opinion concerning how the social world operates. In fact, commonsense beliefs about behavior often are correct. Unfortunately, as has been shown through the scientific study of behavior, human judgment is not always accurate. Scientific methods are not infallible either, but they are designed to minimize the biases that affect subjective opinion. The way in which this is accomplished will be explained in the following chapters.

In this monograph I divide designs into experimental and nonexperimental. The difference between the two concerns the degree to which the experimenter or investigator controls that which he or she studies. The experimental design occurs when the *subjects* (people or social systems) and *conditions* (events or situations) to be studied are manipulated by the investigator. That is, the investigator does something to affect the subjects studied and then determines the effects of those manipulations. Such studies involve a comparison of subject behaviors or characteristics under the various conditions being investigated. The key to experimental design is that the investigator assigns subjects to conditions rather than observing them in naturally occurring situations.

For example, one might design an experimental study to determine if personal tutoring improves student learning. A number or *sample* of students would be located, half being placed into one *treatment group* and half into another. The first treatment group would be given regular instruction while the second would be given regular instruction plus additional personal tutoring. After a period of time, perhaps half the school year, the progress of both groups would be assessed, possibly by comparing school grades. Differences would be attributed to the tutoring, provided that the only difference between the groups in the treatment they received was the tutoring.

The nonexperimental design differs in the degree to which the investigator manipulates subjects and conditions. The investigator may identify conditions, but subjects of the study are not assigned to them. Rather, various observations are made of the subjects who may naturally fall into conditions. In the nonexperimental study of tutoring the investigator would again identify a number of students, but they would only be observed and would not be assigned to conditions. Half the students would be chosen because they were receiving tutoring despite the study, and half would be chosen because they were not. After a reasonable period of time, the progress of the two groups would be compared, perhaps on the same grades as the experimental design subjects. In addition the investigator might administer an achievement test for purposes of the study or collect other data from existing records.

It should be clear from these examples that the nonexperimental study differs from the experimental in the amount of manipulation of subjects and conditions and not in the research question asked or even in the conditions and characteristics studied. Perhaps another example will help illustrate the contrasts.

Experimental designs are perhaps best illustrated by the laboratory experiment. The scientist wishes to determine which of two procedures, products, or treatments results in more of something than the other. For example, he or she might wish to determine if organic fertilizer is superior to inorganic in producing tomatoes. The scientist raises half the subject tomatoes with organic and half with inorganic fertilizer, being careful that the only difference in the treatment of the two groups of plants is the fertilizer. Sunlight, water, type of seed, and spacing are all held constant. He or she raises the plants and determines which had the highest yield of fruit.

This example contains all the elements of the experimental design. The investigator created the two conditions, in this case the fertilization schedule. Subjects were assigned so that half were in one condition and half in the other. All other factors that might differ between the two groups were held constant or controlled. Finally, the subjects were compared on a criterion or characteristic about which the study was conducted.

In contrast, nonexperimental designs utilize observational methods and involve the collection of data with far less direct manipulation of conditions or subjects. In the tomato study one could conduct the same investigation with a nonexperimental design by observing fertilization practices and tomato yields of actual farmers. One might identify two groups of farmers, one that used organic and one that used inorganic fertilizer. One would then gather data, perhaps by asking the farmers directly about yield. Fertilizer use could then be related to tomato yield and conclusions drawn about the efficacy of the two types of fertilizer. Of course there are problems with this study due to the lack of control over extraneous factors. The two types of farmers might differ in more ways than preference for fertilizer. One type might water more, allow less space between plants, or practice a different style of crop rotation. Also one type of farmer might tend to exaggerate reported yields more than the other, thus biasing the data.

It should be apparent that the lack of direct manipulation or control in the nonexperimental design can cause problems in the interpretation of results because the investigator is often unable to assure that extraneous factors, not of concern in the present study, are properly handled. Of course these problems also occur in experimental studies when proper procedures are not or cannot be followed. It should also be noted that the experimental/nonexperimental distinction represents two ends of a continuum rather than two distinct types. There are designs that fall somewhere in between when only partial manipulation is attained. Finally, it is sometimes said that experimental studies establish causal relationships, and nonexperimental studies only establish that two things are related. Although in practice experimental studies are more powerful in their ability to determine that one thing causes another, not all experimental studies establish causation, and not all nonexperimental studies fail to establish it. As mentioned previously, an experimental study can fail to hold constant or control all extraneous factors and would therefore have difficulty in establishing causality. On the other hand, systematic observation, especially over time, can allow powerful causal conclusions, and one should respect the efficacy of these designs. Practically all modern knowledge of astronomy comes from nonexperimental observation.

The beginning student of design might wonder why entire books are devoted to its study. Although the basic principles of design are relatively straightforward, the design of real studies can be extremely complex and difficult. There are many pitfalls and potential biases that may contaminate a study and make it less than conclusive. Considerable knowledge and experience are essential if one plans to conduct good research. Even the nonresearcher who only reads results of studies would do well to understand basic design principles so that he or she can evaluate conclusions drawn from a study. Many times we see in published articles conclusions that seem not to follow from the study described. The reader who is unaware of design principles is at the mercy of an author who might well have overlooked a problem with the design of a study. The individual who wishes to become an accomplished researcher must become an expert in design. The individual who reads results of others' research should learn design principles to be able to form reasonable judgments based on that research.

Plan of the Monograph

The remainder of this monograph will consist of five chapters that present a detailed discussion of experimental and nonexperimental design. Both general concepts and specific applications will be covered. The second chapter presents basic concepts and language for discussions to follow. Some readers may be quite familiar with these concepts and may skip this chapter with no loss in understanding subsequent material. Chapter 3 will be a discussion of design principles in general, pulling together several concepts defined in Chapter 2. In addition this chapter will present pitfalls to the design of good studies. Chapters 4 to 6 cover details of specific designs. Chapter 4 is a discussion of nonexperimental, single-group designs. Chapter 5 presents the multigroup designs, most of which are experimental. Finally, Chapter 6 covers the more complex factorial designs. In each of these three chapters, the advantages and disadvantages of each design are covered, as well as particular pitfalls. Suggestions are offered for minimizing problems with each design, and in many places appropriate statistical procedures for analysis are mentioned. Details of the statistics are beyond the scope of this presentation, and alternative sources are suggested. Several illustrative examples from published studies are included in Chapters 4 to 6 to demonstrate the points made about the specific designs.

2.0 BASIC CONCEPTS

This chapter is concerned with the establishment of basic concepts essential for an understanding of design. In a sense this chapter will provide a language through which later discussions can communicate about design. Included are the concepts of independent and dependent variables, measurement and measurement error, reliability, validity, randomization, control, and generalizability. A thorough understanding of these concepts is essential for achieveing mastery over the remaining material.

Variables

A variable is a qualitative or quantitative entity that can vary or take on different values. In research, variables are the things that are measured and represent the concepts studied. For convenience, variables are often classified as independent or dependent. In most experimental and many nonexperimental designs that deal with determination of causal relationships, it is useful to refer to the causes as independent and the effects as dependent. Sometimes data are collected on several variables, none of which is manipulated and which cannot be classified as cause or effect. In such cases the independent-dependent classification has little meaning, even though the same statistical analyses might be employed as in causal studies.

Perhaps the best example of the independent-dependent dichotomy is illustrated by the laboratory experiment, such as the organic-inorganic fertilizer example of the previous chapter. In this experiment the type of fertilizer (organic and inorganic) was the independent variable because it was directly manipulated by the experimenter and, more important, because it was the putative cause of yield, which was the dependent variable. This independent-dependent categorization would be maintained even if the study were nonexperimental, such as the study of organic using and inorganic using farmers. Again, it is the supposed relationship among the variables that determines variable type and not the experimental nature of the study.

As will be discussed at length in the following chapters, there can be more than two variables in a design, and in fact most studies published today involve multiple variables. The multiple independent variable study is most common, although multiple dependent variable designs have become quite popular in recent years.

Measurement

With any study, variables must be measured in order for analyses to be conducted and conclusions drawn. Measurement is simply the process of assigning numbers to variables that represent attributes or properties of subjects or treatments. The numbers derived through the measurement process can represent convenient labels for discrete categories, such as sex or race, or can represent an underlying measurement continuum for a continuous variable, such as time, length, or scores on an attitude scale. With a discrete variable such as sex, one would arbitrarily assign a number to each possible category, for example, one for males and two for females. The quantification of the discrete variable is a convenience that allows analysis to be conducted. With continuous variables, such as time, the numbers assigned represent amount with smaller numbers generally indicating less of the characteristic than larger numbers. There are actually four types or levels of measurement commonly discussed. For details the interested reader might consult Guilford (1954) or Torgerson (1958).

Measurement Error

Measurement is always accomplished with a specified device or procedure which will be referred to as an instrument. For example, one might measure response latency with a stopwatch, intelligence with a paper-and-pencil test, or education level by asking people how many years of school they completed. No matter what instrument is used, there is always some degree of error associated with it. Error comes from several sources including: the limits of precision of an instrument (a ruler might only be lined in 16ths of an inch), idiosyncratic tendencies of the person using the instrument (the person using the ruler might view it from the side), bias in the design of an instrument (one end of the ruler might be cut off too short), and simple errors in the way a person uses the instrument (a person might erroneously record length).

There are two types of error to be discussed here — random error and bias. Random error occurs when errors are nonsystematic and are as frequently in one direction as the other around the real or true score on the variable. If the theoretical true value is 10, random errors of $+1$ are as likely as -1 so that in the long run there should be as many values of 9 as 11. Bias occurs when the errors tend to be in one direction more than the other. Thus the measurement might always tend to be high. When the true value is 10, most observed values are 11 or 12, with few 10's and fewer 9's. Bias often occurs due to distortions in procedures and characteristics of instruments, observers, and investigators. While bias can occur due to intentional acts on the part of researchers, of particular concern here is bias that is unintentional, arising from instruments and procedures.

Random error causes data collected in a study to be less than precise. However, if one can make certain assumptions about the error component of measurement, one can use statistical procedures to circumvent this problem. Random error implies that deviations from true scores are as likely in either direction. Therefore, if one takes several measurements of a characteristic, the errors of measurement should average out. This is exactly what is done when multiple items are included in a questionnaire or psychological test. While each item itself may be subject to considerable error, averaging scores from several items, each designed to measure the same variable, results in a score in which the random error component averages out to be quite small. I have several times witnessed a class of students estimate the temperature of the classroom. While individual estimates were often off by as much as 10 degrees, the average for the entire class was not off by more than 1 degree, and in fact was probably as accurate as the thermometer against which it was compared.

Bias is far more problematic than random error. Since bias tends to be in one direction, there is no simple process to average out its effects. There may be instances in which it is possible to estimate the magnitude and direction of bias and to adjust for it. Most often investigators attempt to uncover its sources and design instruments or methods to avoid it, and in fact much effort in designing studies involves the avoidance of bias.

Reliability

Reliability is a crucial characteristic of measurement and refers to the consistency of a measuring device. In other words, does the instrument always come up with the same score or number when the true value is the same? For example, if one were to use a ruler to measure the length of a table, reliability would refer to one's ability to always find the same length.

As discussed earlier, measurement is associated with error, and it is the relative magnitude of error to the true or real score that is reliability. Error that is quite small in relationship to true score results in reliable measurement. When errors become large relative to measured characteristics, reliability declines, eventually to the point at which the instrument is worthless. Reliability can be increased by the use of multiple measurements or multiple measures, a strategy frequently adopted in the social sciences. As discussed in the previous section, several measures can be combined, averaging out random error.

Of the several types of reliability, the two most common are discussed here. *Test-retest* involves the continued use of the same instrument to make multiple measurements. Thus one might ask a respondent the same question several times in an interview. *Equivalent forms* refers to the use of different, but equivalent instruments. An example would be asking the same question phrased in different ways. These terms are derived from psychological testing where reliability of tests is established by these as well as other methods.

Validity

Validity of an instrument means that it measures what it is designed to measure. A valid ruler measures length, a valid stopwatch measures time, and a valid intelligence test measures intelligence. Of course validity is not quite this simple because researchers are not always precise in their meanings of concepts and rarely have standards for comparison. For example, a valid measure of socioeconomic status would consist of a composite of income, education level, occupation, and perhaps other variables, as well; but how should they be combined? Should one multiply annual income by education in years or should one add education in years to the hourly rate of pay? How should one quantify occupation — by job level in the organization, by time span of discretion, or by a survey of occupational status?

Validity itself is a simple concept, but the determination of the validity of a measure is elusive. Generally a variable is taken as part of a theoretical framework and establishes that certain hypothesized relationships exist between the instrument and other variables. Thus one might validate a measure of socioeconomic status by showing that the measure is related to certain types of attitudes and behaviors. As one finds that hypothesized relationships are supported, evidence for validity accumulates. When hypotheses are not upheld, either the instrument is invalid or the theories are wrong. Through the collection of evidence over time, a case is built for the validity of measures, which is dependent upon the theoretical models and hypotheses.

Validity and reliability go hand in hand and are two crucial properties of instruments. Their relationship can best be shown with an example. Suppose one has three baseball pitchers and wishes to determine if their pitching is reliable and valid. Reliability is defined as consistency in pitching the ball to the same place each time. Validity is defined as being able to pitch strikes rather than balls. An investigation is set up in which data are collected on each pitcher's performance in several games. The first pitcher always pitches low and outside and walks every batter. In fact, the catcher can predict exactly where the ball will be thrown. This pitcher is perfectly reliable but perfectly invalid. The second pitcher throws a collection of balls and strikes, some high, some low, some inside, and some outside. He is not very reliable, and not very valid either, although he sometimes pitches strikes. The last pitcher throws all strikes — he is both valid and reliable. The principle is this — an instrument can be reliable but not valid, but to be valid an instrument must be reliable. Furthermore, the level of reliability sets a limit to how valid an instrument can be. (See Carmines and Zeller, 1979, for a more thorough treatment of reliability and validity.)

Control

The cornerstone of experimental design is control. It involves holding constant or varying systematically variables so their effects can be removed from a study or compared to other conditions. Control can involve the active manipulation by an investigator of subjects or conditions, or it can involve merely the structuring of an investigation and the manipulation of data. In an experimental design, control usually refers to holding constant the level of a particular variable. Thus one might hold constant or control for sex or intelligence of subjects or time of day in which an experiment is run. This type of control involves the selection of subjects or conditions so their characteristics remain at a constant level or value.

In a nonexperimental study, control can occur by selectively deleting cases that do not have the characteristics of present interest. Suppose one does a study by collecting data from census records. Area of the country, sex of the respondent, type of dwelling, and a host of other variables can be controlled by selecting all cases that are at a certain value for the variables to be controlled. However, there are limits to what can be controlled because there may be crucial variables not collected or available for observation. For example, with census data time of day of the interview or race of the interviewer may not be available and thus could not be controlled. Also, there may be a relationship between the control variables and experimental variables in such a way that one cannot be held constant without the other. In such cases the variables are said to be totally confounded.

Control, then, is holding constant variables not of direct interest in the current investigation so they do not contaminate results. However, once a study is limited to certain values of a control variable, one may not be able to generalize the results to other values. Studies conducted only on women may not yield similar results for men.

One other use of the term *control* is in reference to the control group. Literally, a control group is a group in which values of the independent variable are held at a base or comparison level. When one is comparing a new procedure or process to an old one, the old one represents the control, and the group of subjects in the group comprise the control group. Often the control group is untouched or untreated in an investigation, although they may receive some standard or currently existing treatment or condition. For example, suppose one wished to determine if a particular program was effective in reducing recidivism of convicted felons. One might select two groups of newly released felons, an experimental group that receives the program and a control group that does not. The study would involve a comparison of the two groups.

Randomization

The concept of randomization has already been discussed in the sense of random errors of measurement. With measurement this referred to the fact that positive errors were as likely as negative. With experimental design, randomization refers to the assignment of subjects to conditions or levels of an independent variable — either by the investigator or by a natural process in the field.

If there are several levels of an independent variable, which might be represented by several treatment groups (one or more of which might be a control group), randomization means that each subject in the study had an equal chance or probability of falling into each group.

Randomization in a sense is a process opposite from control. Where controlling means holding the value of certain variables constant, randomization means letting the value run freely. The intent is that, through random assignment of subjects to groups, the effects of uncontrolled subject variables will cancel out. With the convicted felon example, one might suspect that the reaction of younger felons will be different from older felons but not wish to include age as a variable for study. If the age distribution of the two groups differed, it would be difficult to determine if age alone accounted for the results. To control for age one might hold it constant by choosing as subjects only those felons between certain age limits. Alternately, all felons could be randomly assigned to the program and control group, assuming that the two groups will be about equivalent on age. Of course, one could test this assumption by comparing ages between the groups.

Confounding

The best way to describe confounding is with an example. Suppose an investigator is interested in determining the relationship between achievement test scores and average family income among Mexican-Americans. The problem is that achievement scores are probably related to or confounded with education level. It would be difficult to determine whether achievement or education was the crucial variable if a relationship was found. That is, suppose people with high school diplomas tended to get better jobs and also tended to have higher scores. It would not follow necessarily that achievement was the causal factor. Perhaps it was just the diploma, independent of achievement, that resulted in better employment and more income.

Often in studies, both experimental and nonexperimental, there are variables related to variables of interest which distort or confound the results. With experiments they might be related to the independent variable so that both are actually manipulated. In such cases one does not know which of the two was responsible for the observed levels of the dependent variable. Well-designed studies are able to handle this confounding, as will be shown throughout this monograph.

Generalizability of Results

At the end of any study or investigation there arises the question of generalizability of results. That is, do the results found in the present study hold as well for other samples of subjects at other locations? Studies in the social sciences are rarely, if ever, universal, and one must keep in mind the limitations. A particular study may be limited only to males, certain areas of the country, certain cultures, or the subjects chosen. The variables included, the particular controls used, and the way in which subjects are assigned to treatments all determine the limits to generalizability.

Campbell and Stanley (1963) discuss at great length factors which limit the internal and external validity of studies. Internal validity refers to the generalization of conclusions within a given study itself. That is, given the structure of a particular investigation, can valid conclusions be drawn? In other words can one state that the independent variable caused the dependent variable or are there confounding factors that prevent conclusions? External validity is generalization beyond the current study and sample. Given that there is internal validity, do the results generalize to other samples?

It is both confounding and the design structure of an investigation that determine whether it is internally valid. Campbell and Stanley (1963) discuss many sources of invalidity including: (1) instrument reactivity — the effects instruments have on the subjects in a study; (2) history — things that may happen to subjects over time that have nothing to do with the study; (3) unreliability of instruments; (4) differential subject loss over time in various groups; (5) bias in the assignment of subjects to treatment groups; and (6) instrument changes over time.

External validity is compromised when conditions in the investigation differ from those in the generalization. Examples of factors leading to external invalidity include: (1) reactivity of instrumentation — effects caused by use of instruments; (2) Hawthorne effects — effect on subjects of knowing they are in an experiment; (3) invalidity of instruments; and (4) confounding characteristics of the particular samples, that is, the samples chosen might not adequately represent the population to which results are to be generalized. The best example is the use of college students for studies generalized to the U.S. population as a whole.

In this chapter we have established some basic concepts essential for the understanding of design. The reader at this point should have a general feel for the major design principles. One should be aware that a design involves structuring the measurement of variables in such a way that their relationships can be determined. When the study is conducted, data are collected on the variables and are analyzed with statistical methods. At many places in the following chapters specific statistical techniques will be suggested for particular designs, and references will be provided for the reader interested in more detail. Statistics is a topic essential for study by the serious researcher, and it goes hand in hand with a study of design. While design involves the structure of a study, statistics deals with analysis of the data generated and the drawing of conclusions from that data.

3.0 BASIC LOGIC OF DESIGN

The major purpose of any design is to answer some specific research question utilizing well-developed principles of scientific inquiry. The basic ideas of design are reasonably simple and straightforward, but the design of actual social science investigations is often quite complex and difficult due to several factors including: limitations on the degree of control an investigator can exert over human beings and social systems, poorly formulated concepts, instruments of limited validity, complex interrelationships among large numbers of variables, and lack of well-developed and validated theoretical models. Research questions are often imprecise, instruments to measure variables are often unavailable, and simple relationships among variables seem quite elusive.

Any investigation requires several steps to complete. First, the investigator must formulate a researchable question. This question may be in the form of a hypothesis that certain relationships exist among variables, or it may be of an exploratory nature, essentially asking what is the relationship among variables. A research question may begin in a loosely formulated form, but must eventually be stated such that a testable hypothesis or model is generated. The more precise the question, the easier it will be to answer, and if asked precisely enough, the remaining steps will fall more easily into place. Of course, one must certainly avoid formulating questions that are so narrow as to be of no practical or scientific significance, but to formulate meaningful questions requires experience and considerable knowledge of a content area.

The second step is to plan the design of the investigation. This step involves choice of variables, procedures, controls, and randomization plans. At this point one must decide whether the design will be experimental or nonexperimental and whether the study will take place in a laboratory or field setting. Decisions must be made about where and how to collect the data, and which variables are to be controlled, at what level, and with what methods? If subjects are assigned to levels of the independent variable, some procedure must be chosen for assignment. Once the basic design is laid out, careful consideration should be given to possible confounding variables. If variables are identified as possible confounds, a strategy should be chosen to deal with them. General procedures will be discussed at a later point in this chapter.

The third step, which may occur at the same time as the second, involves selection of instruments for dependent variables, and *operationalization* of independent variables, which is essentially the statement of procedures used to create their levels. Choice of instruments is as important as any step in an investigation, but too often little attention is given to instrumentation. This is especially true in experimental laboratory studies where considerable effort might be put into operationalizing levels of the independent variable, but little is given to measuring the dependent variable. Too often an investigator spends much time and energy developing a complex manipulation for the independent variable, but only spends a few moments creating self-report items of unknown reliability and untested validity to measure the dependent variable.

The fourth and final step of any study is simply to conduct it. It is always best to carefully design a study and then to carry it out as planned, but often unforeseen problems arise and modifications are made to the original plan. Instruments are sometimes revised until they are sensitive to manipulations of independent variables, and sometimes procedures are modified when conditions change. If these things occur, it is always best to replicate the study so that more confidence can be placed in the results and the conclusions.

Much has been written about all four of these steps. The present topic is research design, which is step 2. The remainder of this chapter will limit itself to the design aspect.

Experimental Studies

For the most part, experimental studies are considered to be more powerful than nonexperimental designs in uncovering causal relationships among variables. This is due to the fact that through control and randomization, potential confounding effects can be removed from a study. A nonexperimental study merely establishes that relationships exist among variables. However, through systematic observation over time, and collection of data on several variables, it is indeed possible to determine cause and effect. Experimental studies which involve direct manipulation are more frequently conclusive because they involve principles of control, randomization, and comparison.

In a sense an experimental design can be viewed as a trade-off among comparison, randomization, and control. Some variables are set at different levels and compared, others are held at a constant level and controlled, and still others may be free to vary with the hope that randomization will average out confounds. In the perfect experiment the independent variables are manipulated, subjects are randomly assigned, and all other variables are held constant. The investigator identifies a set of variables and makes a decision whether he wishes to manipulate (treat as independent) or hold constant (control) each variable. Of course when he controls a variable by holding it constant, he limits generalizability to only the chosen level. If he treats a variable as independent, he determines its effects on the dependent variable, as well as its relationship to other independent variables in the study.

If one had unlimited time, subjects, and resources, one could include any number of independent variables in a study. However, the more independent variables included in a study, the more subjects needed to fill conditions, the more data collected on those subjects, and the more complex the analysis and interpretation. Thus there are practical limits to the number of independent variables that can be included in a study. Hence, control by holding variables constant is essential.

Of course, rather than holding values of a variable constant, one can let them vary and randomly assign those values to the different levels of the independent variables. This method is most often used by assigning subjects at random to conditions. However, it is not always practical or appropriate to randomly assign values to variables, especially when the variables in question are related to the experimental conditions. These situations undoubtedly call for some sort of control, and sometimes this can be accomplished systematically. For example, in a laboratory experiment it is common practice to mix up the order in which conditions are run. Sometimes this is done by alternating, or *counterbalancing,* a procedure to be discussed later in this monograph.

As discussed previously, confounding occurs when a variable not of immediate interest in a study is related to variables in the study. These confounding variables can be related to experimental conditions or treatments or to subject characteristics when these are the independent variables in the study. An example of the latter situation is the failure to definitively answer the controversial and highly explosive question about racial differences in abilities. The race variable is so confounded with social and economic variables that racial comparisons of intelligence test scores are inconclusive.

Confounding of subject characteristics can be handled by randomly assigning subjects to groups or by choosing subjects at the same level of the confounding variable. This latter approach is often difficult because it may be hard to find enough subjects with the necessary characteristics, because the confounding variable itself may be related to a host of other variables, and because there might be prohibitions against such choices.

Confounding of treatment variables can be handled through careful design and planning of a study. However, there are instances when two variables are confounded in such a way that it is impossible to completely separate them in a single study. For example, suppose one wished to compare two interactive teaching methods on learning. Students would be randomly assigned to the two methods and would be subsequently tested for knowledge of the subject with a standard achievement test. Now suppose one method produces more student responses in a unit of time than the other. Method 1 might require two responses per minute while method 2 requires four. Number of subject responses would be confounded with treatment and may alone account for learning differentials. One could equate number of responses by making the sessions with method 1 twice as long as with method 2. Unfortunately, now duration of training is confounded with treatment. One would have to make a choice about which confound is the most damaging and control it at the expense of the other. The only way out would be to somehow redesign the teaching methods so they produce the same frequency of response. Otherwise, interpretations of the efficacy of the two methods could only be made in terms of the confounding variable. More research would have to be conducted with the frequency variable to determine its role in learning.

Nonexperimental Studies

Perhaps the most important difference between the experimental and nonexperimental study is subject assignment. In the experimental design, the researcher assigns subjects (optimally at random) to conditions or levels of the independent variable, but in the nonexperimental study there is no assignment. Often creation of the levels of independent variables is another difference, but an experimental design does not require that the investigator create the levels of the independent variable — he or she merely assigns subjects and observes results. When subject assignment does not occur, the study is nonexperimental even if a treatment is created.

For example, one might ask the question whether compensatory education improves college grades for low-income students. One might identify a group of low-income students and assign half of them to an existing program and half to a no-treatment control group. College grades would be the dependent variable, and the design would be experimental. On the other hand, one might be active in designing a compensatory education program which a number of students would attend. One could collect data on college grades of these students as well as a group who did not attend. However, without assignment, the study is nonexperimental. The fact that the investigator created the program is irrelevant. The design itself is not concerned with who created the independent variable. Rather it is concerned with the structure of the investigation, and from this structure, inferences can be drawn.

Although in a nonexperimental study there is no assignment of subjects, many of the other principles of research design still apply. Control over levels of certain variables can be exerted, but control does not involve active manipulation of conditions. Rather control can be exercised in the selection of cases to include in the observational study. Cases can be chosen to meet certain specified criteria, such as selecting only males, only people below a certain annual income, or organizations in the nonprofit sector. Control is achieved by selecting only certain values of control variables and observing the variables of interest.

Statistical procedures are also available to help control the effects of certain variables. Although these procedures are based on certain assumptions which may not always be true, it is possible to statistically adjust for or control the effects of certain variables. If one is interested in studying the relationship between income and political party preference, one might simply correlate income level with party membership. However, education is related to income and education alone might be related to preference, independent of income. Education level can be controlled by selecting only those subjects who are at a certain level, perhaps high school graduates. The correlation between income and membership can also be statistically adjusted for education using partial correlation. This would indicate whether there is a relationship remaining between income and membership after removing the common relationship among all three variables.

It is often taught that only experiments can establish causal relationships among variables and that observational or correlational studies can only establish that relationships exist without specifying causal direction. While in practice this is often true, one should be cautious in assuming that experimental designs always establish causality and observational studies do not. Many experimental designs are so fraught with confounding variables that causal inferences cannot be made with reasonable confidence, and there are nonexperimental, observational designs that can establish causal chains of events.

Going back to the income-party preference example, suppose one hypothesized that income causes party preference through some theoretical process. Merely showing that Republicans have higher incomes than Democrats would not convince any social scientist that the hypothesis was correct. However, one could make systematic observations over time and compile quite convincing evidence. One could identify a large sample of young high school graduates and track their income and party membership for the following 20 years. If those individuals with higher initial incomes became Republicans and those with lower initial incomes became Democrats, and if party membership shifted with income, one would have strong evidence for the hypothesis. Observing the close correspondence of the two variables over time with income change almost always preceding party change would be convincing and indicate a causal connection. Of course other variables would certainly be involved, but these could be observed as well, and a theory of party preference might be validated.

Problems with Internal and External Validity

In the previous chapter there was brief mention of internal and external validity and design problems that threaten each. Such problems, which arise from confounding variables within a design, have been extensively covered by Campbell and his colleagues (e.g., Campbell and Stanley, 1963; Cook and Campbell, 1979). Variables that are related to the independent variables may account for observed differences in the dependent variable, giving the false appearance of a valid answer to a research question. The astute researcher is aware of the possible sources of these invalidating influences on results and guards against them in planning designs. Specific sources are covered below.

History. There are events that may affect subjects in addition to the independent variables or conditions of interest. For example, one might design a study to see if the 55 mile per hour speed limit reduced traffic fatalities. Data on traffic deaths before and after the limit was introduced could be collected and might show that deaths declined. However, it might also be discovered that due to higher gasoline prices, people drove fewer miles. If differences in fatality rates were found, it would be difficult to separate the effects of speed limit from the effects of mileage.

Instrument Reactivity. It is an established principle of measurement that instruments react with the things they measure. In some cases the reactivity is small relative to the variable measured and is inconsequential, but in other cases it may totally distort measurement. In nuclear physics the principle of uncertainty is a statement of the fact that measurement of subatomic particles is never exact because instruments disturb the particles being measured. In the social sciences it is often difficult to know when reactivity is severe enough to be problematic. It may affect someone's attitudes to fill out an attitude questionnaire, and it may change behavior when a person knows he is being observed. Furthermore, there is a vast literature on the effects an experimenter can have on the behavior of subjects, many of which would be considered instrument reactions.

Instrument reactivity occurs in two ways. First, instruments directly affect subjects so that true measurements are distorted. In other words the instrument disturbs that which is measured. Second, instruments may interact with treatments so that subject responses to various treatments are changed and differ from treatment to treatment. As long as the former distortion is constant, comparisons among variables can be made, although with increased error. The latter situation may totally distort results and confound a study.

Perhaps the best way to deal with instrument reactivity is to test for its effects within a design. That is, the design would be structured to include a test for instrument reactivity. The best example is the Solomon four-group design where a dependent variable is measured after application of the independent variable, and half the subjects receive an additional preindependent variable measurement while half do not. A comparison of these two groups on the measurement after intervention would be a test for reactivity of the pretest and its possible interaction with the independent variable.

Unreliability of Instruments. This problem was discussed previously in the section on reliability. When instruments are unreliable, it becomes difficult to draw firm conclusions from a study because the variance among subjects becomes too large. The best solution for unreliability is to improve the instrument, find another, or take multiple measurements with the same or equivalent instruments. Using large samples can also help as the large errors of measurement may average out. However, if an instrument is too unreliable, it will lack any validity and be totally worthless.

Invalidity of Instruments. This is an obvious problem since an invalid instrument does not measure the variable of interest. However, it is not always easy to determine when an instrument is invalid. If one can define precisely what is to be measured and can derive hypotheses concerning the behavior of the measured characteristic, one can validate an instrument against those hypotheses. For example, if one were to develop an instrument to measure mathematical ability, one could validate it against the hypotheses that individuals high on this characteristic, in comparison to low scorers, would receive better grades in mathematics courses, score higher on standardized mathematics achievement tests, and make more successful statisticians. If these hypotheses were not supported empirically, one would question whether the instrument could really measure the characteristic in question. The only solution to invalidity is to develop or find an instrument that is valid.

Instrument Change Over Time. This problem refers to an instrument's changing validity over time, termed temporal invalidity by Chubb (1978), who demonstrated the phenomenon with a political cynicism questionnaire. In this case subjects changed their perceptions of the questions over an eight-year period. Instrument changes are not limited to shifts in subject characteristics. For example, in interview studies, interviewers may improve their technique with practice and later interviews might be more valid than earlier interviews due to improved interviewer skills. The best way to handle this problem is to be certain that collection of data among levels of the independent variable is not systematic. That is, data should not be collected first for one level and then for another. Also, checks should be made on the instrument periodically to be sure its characteristics have not changed.

Differential Subject Loss. In many studies that take place over time, subjects may be lost due to refusal to continue or to events that preclude continuation, such as injury or death. This problem is of concern for two reasons. First, attrition may not be random and completers might be different from noncompleters, a situation that would limit generalizability of results. Second, if attrition differs among treatment groups, it may be difficult to know if attrition alone accounted for results.

Solutions to this problem go beyond design considerations and involve selecting procedures that assure continued subject participation, such as payment, preliminary commitment, and selecting elapsed time to be as short as possible between the beginning and end of a study.

Bias in Assignment of Subjects to Treatments. This problem has already been discussed; it represents a breakdown in random assignment. It is always best to randomly assign subjects to levels of the independent variable, but when this is not possible, one should attempt to control as much as possible all differences among groups. This could be done by selecting matched subjects for each group. Matching variables might include personal characteristics, demographic characteristics, scores on pretests, and specific behaviors such as arrest records or school grades. One can also use statistical methods to control for differences, but these procedures are not attractive alternatives to matching or random assignment.

Hawthorne Effects. Hawthorne effects, named from the well-known Western Electric studies in industry (Roethlisberger and Dickson, 1939), refer to the distortion in behavior that occurs when people know they are subjects of a study. This effect is somewhat akin to instrument reactivity, but it does not have to involve the instrument itself. That is, the mere knowledge that one is in a study may affect behavior even if observations are not being made. Procedures to control this problem are: unobtrusive studies in which subjects are unaware they are being studied, telling control subjects they are also in an experiment even if they are to receive no manipulation, and allowing an adaptation period during which no observations are made.

Nonrepresentative Samples. This problem is mainly one of generalization when the samples chosen are so specialized that conclusions can only be made to a limited population, in some cases not beyond the original sample itself. For example, much research in psychology has been criticized for its generalization from male subjects to humans in general in light of frequent findings of sex differences in behavior. In addition, most psychological studies have been done in the United States, and since most subjects are college students, many findings may well be limited to an American college student population. Solutions to this problem are to choose samples that represent the population to which generalizations are to be made. This may require replication of studies using various samples in different areas of the United States, as well as other countries.

Design Notation

The remainder of this monograph will be concerned with specific designs and the application of the principles discussed to this point. The various designs are best explained diagrammatically. Hence, for all but the most complex designs, a notation system will be used that is based on Campbell and Stanley (1963). In this system, observations or measurements of variables are represented by O's. Applications of the independent variables or treatments are X's. The time sequence of O's and X's in the design run from left to right. For example, three observations, each immediately following one of three sequential treatments for a single group of subjects would be diagramed as:

$$X_1 \; O_1 \; X_2 \; O_2 \; X_3 \; O_3.$$

For two groups each receiving the same treatments but in a different order the structure would be:

$$X_1 \; O_1 \; X_2 \; O_2 \; X_3 \; O_3.$$

$$X_2 \; O_1 \; X_3 \; O_2 \; X_1 \; O_3.$$

Each row represents a separate treatment group, but not necessarily a separate condition. The subscripts on the treatments are labels to distinguish among them. The subscripts on the observations indicate the order in which they are made.

4.0 ONE-GROUP DESIGNS

One-group designs are all considered nonexperimental since they do not involve assignment of subjects to conditions. Rather a single group of subjects is observed, although the investigator may create a treatment condition. There are three designs that will be covered in this chapter, although these three can be expanded to more complex designs involving a single group. These are the most basic designs involving a single group, and they are popular throughout the social sciences because of their simplicity and ease of application.

Pretest-Posttest Design

The pretest-posttest design involves two measurements of the dependent variable surrounding, in time, the administration or occurrence of a single treatment or level of the independent variable. Its structure in the notation of the previous chapter is:

$$O_1 \; X \; O_2.$$

In this design subjects serve as their own control, and comparisons are made before and after treatment. An assumption is made that differences between pretest and posttest are due to the effects of the treatment that occurred in the middle.

The most obvious shortcoming of this design is that one cannot be certain that some factor or event other than the treatment was responsible for posttest change. This problem is especially acute where the time period between pretest and posttest is long and when the researcher has limited control over events occurring to the subjects. For example, suppose one were to conduct a study to determine if a media campaign would increase the frequency of voter registrations in a particular city. A pretest could be taken of the number of registrations one month prior to the campaign, and a posttest one month after the campaign. However, a host of other events might transpire in the middle, such as emergence of a heated issue in the community or the intensification of a campaign. With this design it would be impossible to determine which factor or factors were responsible for increased registrations. A colleague of mine was involved in an evaluation of a state police crackdown on drunk driving. Accident records were gathered before and after implementation of the crackdown. Unfortunately, the crackdown occurred just as the state adopted a 55 mile per hour speed limit, destroying the possibility of drawing definitive conclusions.

This design is also sensitive to instrument reactivity and Hawthorne effects. Since there are no comparison groups, it is difficult to separate the effects of treatment from the effects of measurement or knowledge of being in an experiment. Hawthorne effects are especially problematic when the pretest is taken before the subjects know about the study. Conditions then change from pretest to posttest beyond the treatment of interest. Instrument reactivity is a special problem when it involves treatment-instrument interaction. In many cases the pretest might sensitize subjects to aspects of the treatment to which they might not otherwise react. In other words the pretest cues subjects about the treatment and enables them to guess what the investigator is expecting. These problems can be minimized by careful selection of instruments to be minimally reactive and by assuring that any reactivity is constant from pretest to posttest. For Hawthorne effects this would involve informing subjects before the pretest about the study, thus holding that knowledge constant.

The structure of this design is simple, and simple procedures can handle the data this design generates. Most commonly, dependent t tests are used to test for statistical significance from pretest to posttest (Winer, 1971).

The one-group pretest-posttest is not one of the better designs available due to the rather severe limitations already described. It is a rather simple design to use, but it is strongly advised that a more conclusive design be used whenever possible. This design is often utilized for program evaluations where the goal is to determine the effectiveness of a particular program. Many times with such activities, control or comparison groups are unavailable, requiring the use of this design or no design.

Interrupted Time Series

This design is similar to the pretest-posttest except that there are more than two measurements. Ideally, there are an equal number of measurement periods before and after treatment, and the period between measurements is constant. These designs can range from several to hundreds of measurements, with the number determining what types of analyses can be conducted.

This design is found in two applications. First, it is a direct extention of the pretest-posttest with more than two measurements. The second use is when periodic data exist over a considerable length of time, and the purpose of the investigation is to determine whether the variables of interest changed at a specified point in the series. This second use is generally considered to be a time series, although a broader use of the term is taken here. Several examples of time series are:

$$O_1 \ O_2 \ O_3 \ X \ O_4 \ O_5 \ O_6$$

$$O_1 \ X \ O_2 \ O_3 \ O_4$$

$$O_1 \ O_2 \ldots O_{50} \ X \ O_{51} \ O_{52} \ldots O_{100}$$

The multiple pretest-posttest designs are an improvement over the single pretest-posttest. The advantage with this design is that it allows determination of trends over time, that is, the slope of the graph of the dependent variable over time. This trend estimate is important because it might well be that the posttest level of a dependent variable is at exactly the place one would expect, based on previous observations over time. The dependent variable might show an increase, decrease, or cyclical change over time without treatment or intervention. This is especially true with aggregate data based on naturally occurring social units. Traffic accident rates, crime rates, and unemployment rates all show trends over time having causes that lie outside of most studies. Techniques have been developed to determine trends in data and estimate whether a discontinuity occurred at a specified location in the series.

Procedures to analyze time series data can become quite complex and most social scientists receive little exposure to them in graduate school. For long series with 50 measurements or more, complex mathematical modeling procedures have been developed that can well describe the form of the series and uncover any changes that may have occurred. Perhaps the most powerful technique is the autoregressive integrated moving average (ARIMA), which indicates complex trends in a time series (see McDowall, McCleary, Meidinger and Hay, 1980, for details).

For a smaller number of measurements, other less complex and powerful procedures must be used. Certainly the analysis of variance is available when there are a few retestings. However, there would be too many group means to compare as the number of retestings becomes large. Swaminathan and Algina (1977) have developed multiple regression procedures which allow a comparison of regression lines before and after treatment.

While the multiple testing designs are certainly more powerful than the single pretest-posttest, they do suffer from most of the same shortcomings. Again the major problem is lack of control for history. One can never be certain that some event other than the treatment in question caused the change in dependent variable. The advantage of the time series is that one can see the direction in which trends were heading at the time of intervention or treatment. A treatment might inhibit or stop a trend which would not be reflected in a single pretest-posttest comparison. Therefore, the multiple-measurement design provides somewhat stronger evidence for treatment effects.

Instrument reactivity and Hawthorne effects are in some ways attenuated and in some ways compounded. Many instruments, if administered several times, might show declining validity and reliability due to boredom and fatigue on the part of subjects. Distortions may occur because subjects attempt to be consistent over time when they know they are being studied. On the other hand subjects may adapt to being part of an investigation and give more natural responses after an initial adjustment period.

Time series studies may be especially subject to instrument change over time since measurements may take place over many months or years. In fact it is not unusual to find historical studies utilizing data from previous centuries. However, with such data, procedures for collection may change over time. Once I attempted to gather time series data on the number of admissions to state psychiatric hospitals between 1978 and 1980 in one of the southern states. Due to changes in definition of admissions, it was impossible to acquire equivalent data for the entire period from the records. So much more severe are the problems in acquiring good data over longer periods of time. ARIMA requires a minimum of 50 measurement periods, which would require half a century of data if annual rates are of interest. Such studies that cannot utilize previously collected data are quite time consuming and are not often undertaken.

Correlational Designs

Included with the other one-group studies are correlational designs which are purely observational. That is, the investigator does not intervene in any way or expose subjects to a manipulation. Rather measurements are taken on a group of individuals or social entities, and relationships are determined among the measures. These measurements can be taken through direct observation, questionnaires, or existing records. They may be repeated over time, a procedure that makes this approach quite powerful. In this section both the one-measurement cross-sectional design and the multiple-measurement longitudinal design will be covered.

Cross-sectional Design. The simplest of the correlational designs is the cross-sectional in which all measurements are taken at one point in time. The structure of the design would be simply:

O

where O represents all observations on all variables. This design is extremely popular due to its simplicity and ease of administration. It requires nothing more than the collection of two or more measures on a set of subjects or social entities at one point in time and requires no treatments or manipulations. A well-conducted study can involve time-consuming development of instruments, but many use existing measures or collect data from available records. Such studies can sometimes be completed in a single day.

Cross-sectional designs are especially attractive in field studies where control over subjects is quite difficult to acquire. In fact, probably most field studies utilize this design because of its simplicity and ease of conducting.

The cross-sectional approach is quite useful in determining if two or more variables are related, and often establishment of relationships is the extent of a research question. When there are more than two variables in a study, it may become difficult to tease out complex interrelationships. For two variables one can calculate the correlation coefficient as an index of strength of relationship and test it for statistical significance. With three or more variables, more complex data-analytic procedures are possible.

When one has several variables, the interest might be in determining whether one can construct a smaller number of dimensions or factors which does an adequate job of explaining the original, larger set. Procedures such as factor analysis are dimension-reduction techniques developed to determine the underlying theoretical factors among a set of variables. The interested reader is referred to any of a number of sources on the topic including Kim and Mueller (1978) and Rummel (1970).

If one can assume that certain variables are caused or preceded by others, one can use multiple regression to derive a functional relationship between the two sets. With multiple regression one predicts a criterion or dependent variable from a set of predictor or independent variables. Equations are generated of the form:

$$y = b_0 + b_1x_1 + \ldots + b_nx_n$$

where y is the dependent variable, the x's are independent variables, and the b's are constants. The x's and y are observed; the b's are calculated from the data (see Lewis-Beck, 1980, for a more complete treatment of multiple regression).

Multiple regression can be used for theory testing and can provide weak support for causal models. Such regression procedures fall under the rubric of path analysis, which is a means of using cross-sectional, correlational data to examine likely causal connections among variables. Using correlations and regression coefficients, one compares observed results to those predicted by a model. Finding that set of results is evidence in support of the model, but is consistent with other possible models as well. For details on path analysis, see Asher (1976).

One way to improve the ability of cross-sectional studies to yield causal data would be to take some measurement at a later point in time. Such a design would be represented as:

O O'

where O and O' represent observations of different variables. Such designs fall somewhat between the truly cross-sectional and the longitudinal — they take place over time, but only a single measurement is made on each variable. In such designs variables predicted to be causes are measured first, followed in time by variables expected to be effects. For example, I conducted a study of employee turnover to test a causal model hypothesizing that certain organizational and personal employee characteristics would lead to job dissatisfaction, which would lead to intentions of quitting, which would lead to actual turnover. Although the ideal design would have been to lag all four steps in the causal chain, the final variable, turnover, was collected after the other variables. This procedure made it difficult to argue that turnover could have caused the variables measured before it. Of course this study, while supporting the causal model, in no way provided proof that it was correct.

Perhaps the major shortcoming of the cross-sectional design is that it only establishes relationships, although path analysis can be used to provide a weak test of causal relationships. For the purely cross-sectional study with all measures taken at the same time, history is of little consequence. That is, there is probably little that can happen within the short time span of data collection that can distort results. However, when some of the variables are measured at a later time, it is possible that intervening events caused spurious relationships. For example, suppose in the turnover study, those employees who were dissatisfied and intending to quit all expressed their feelings and were given raises and concessions to get them to stay. It might well have happened that the concessions changed the normal sequence of events, and no support would have been found for the model.

A more serious problem in the correlational design is instrument reactivity. Of particular concern is *common method variance* in studies that make use of one procedure for collecting data, most commonly the self-report questionnaire or interview. Subject response tendencies and bias when responding to requests for self-report may account for false relationships that are found. People may report attitudes and behaviors in a manner that is more consistent than they are in reality. This tendency toward consistency can enhance correlation coefficients. The component of the correlation due to bias common to the method of data collection would be the *common method variance*. Studies that utilize several modes of data collection, or collect data in a way that assures noninteraction of measures, are more powerful.

Hawthorne effects can also be a problem with the cross-sectional study for much the same reason as instrument reactivity. People who know they are in a study may distort their responses for a number of reasons including a desire to look good or provide good data for the investigator. Some procedures are available to help identify certain biases such as faking and social desirability bias. Subjects found to exhibit biases might be eliminated from the sample. Of course elimination of subjects may limit generalizability to only subjects who do not distort results.

Longitudinal Designs. A variation of the correlational study is the longitudinal or panel design which involves two or more measurements of variables in a study taken on the same group of subjects. Its structure is:

$$O_1 \, O_2 \ldots O_n$$

where the O's represent measurements on all variables. This approach is more powerful than the cross-sectional due to the lagging procedure explained above. That is, it is possible to observe over time if certain values of a variable at one point are associated with certain values of another variable at a different point.

The simplest example of a longitudinal design is the cross-lagged panel design with two variables, each measured twice (see Kenny and Harackiewicz, 1979, for details). Such a design is shown in Figure 4.1, where variables income and education are each measured at age 25 and age 50 for a group of subjects. There are six possible correlations: the correlation of each variable with itself across time and the correlations of income with education within the same time period and across time periods. Of particular interest are these last four coefficients. If one hypothesizes that education is a strong cause of income, but income is at best a weak cause of education, one would expect that income at age 25 would show a weak correlation with education at 50, but education at 25 would show a relatively strong relationship to income at age 50. Furthermore, one would expect little correlation between income and education at 25, but a strong relationship at age 50. This pattern provides support for causal hypotheses, somewhat stronger than a cross-sectional study using path analysis. However, with no control over these variables, the support is weak as there are many alternative explanations for these results.

Longitudinal designs can involve far more than two variables and measurement periods can be quite long. Of course with many variables and measurements, the data analysis becomes complex and difficult. Such studies are not frequent in the social sciences, perhaps due to their complexity and the difficulty of studying individuals over a long time span.

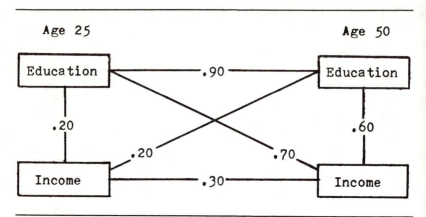

Figure 4.1 Cross-Lagged Panel Design
Note: Hypothetical correlations are indicated, illustrating that education at age 25 might cause income at age 50.

History can become quite a problem for longitudinal designs since there are no controls for outside events, although often it might be just those events that are of interest. That is, the goal of a study might be to ascertain if the relationship between variables changes over time as a function of historical events. Unfortunately, with this type of design, one would never be certain what events caused changes in relationships.

Instrument reactivity and Hawthorne effects may also pose problems for the same reasons as with other one-group designs. Again, multiple testings may attenuate or accentuate these problems.

Examples

Pretest-Posttest Design. The one-group pretest-posttest design is well-illustrated by an organizational study reported by Frederiksen (1978). This was an applied study intended to evaluate the effectiveness of behavioral problem solving and participation in reorganization. The study was undertaken at a Veterans Administration outpatient clinic in response to recognized problems with patient dropout, long waiting lists, and long time periods between appointments.

A pretest-posttest design was chosen with data collected on several important variables including proportion of new patients seen, dropout rate, and interappointment interval. The reorganization was designed by the professional staff utilizing a behavioral problem-solving approach. Results showed significant decreases in dropout (52 vs. 26%), time on waiting list (22 vs. 8 days), and interappointment interval (25 vs. 11 days). These results were taken for support of the effectiveness of the intervention.

While this study is certainly clear in showing that changes occurred, the lack of control makes results difficult to interpret. Of particular concern is that the expressed goal of the study was to evaluate the particular intervention strategy. Unfortunately, while one can state that the intended effects occurred, one cannot be certain specifically what caused them. That is, the same effects might have occurred through use of other techniques for reorganization. Furthermore, there may well have been factors occurring at the time of intervention that in fact accounted for the change. Finally, the application of this procedure to only one organization makes generalization to other sites difficult. Overall, the results of this study are quite suggestive of the efficacy of the behavioral problem-solving approach in organizations. However, the results are merely suggestive and are quite limited. They need to be replicated in other organizations and under more controlled conditions. A comparison of this approach with others, including reorganization with no staff involvement, would provide a more meaningful evaluation. However, as a first step, this study was useful and provided interesting data at relatively little investment of resources.

Interrupted Time Series. There are many examples of time series studies in the program evaluation literature. The one chosen here was conducted by Mazur-Hart and Berman (1977) to determine if no-fault divorce laws tend to increase the number of divorces. This study asked a simple question and used a simple design. Its concern was whether the divorce rate for a particular state increased after implementation of no-fault divorce. The design was an interrupted time series.

This study was conducted in Nebraska about four years after implementation of a new no-fault law. Public divorce records provided the data which consisted of monthly total divorces for the state. Data were analyzed for 41 months before and 29 months after the law went into effect.

The data were first analyzed to determine if autocorrelation existed among the observations. Since it did not, it was felt that multiple regression would be preferable to the more complex ARIMA. The purpose of the regression analysis was to determine if there were any changes in the divorce rate trend from the period before to the period after implementation of the new law. The data showed an upward trend during the entire period; that is, the divorce rate drifted upward for the entire series. There was no discontinuity or change in trend around the time of intervention. Thus the conclusion was that the new law had no effect on divorce rate, a conclusion that failed to support the contentions of the law's critics who felt that it would encourage divorce.

Of course there are obvious limitations to this study since it was nonexperimental and failed to control for invalidating factors. First, there was no control for history, and many other events might have occurred at the time of the law's implementation that would have suppressed the divorce rate. Of course, in defense of the design it seems unlikely that such effects would have occurred at exactly the same time as the new law and would have exactly canceled out its effects. This problem would have been more severe had the series shown a change which might have had several causes.

Perhaps a bigger limitation of this study was that it was conducted only in a single state. The one-sample nature of the study makes premature generalization risky until replication can confirm these results in other settings.

However, overall this study was a well-conducted time series in that the research question was clearly formulated, appropriate data were located, and sufficient observations were taken on either side of the intervention. Thus it provided useful data about the likely effects, or lack thereof, of no-fault divorce laws on divorce rates.

Correlational Design. An example of a correlational design has been conducted by O'Malley (1975). The interesting feature, making it an obvious example of this design, is that it was a retrospective study of suicide in Australia during World War II. Its purpose was to validate a theory relating suicide to war. Specifically, it was proposed that the more severe the threat to a population, the more social integration within the population, and the less the suicide rate. Thus the closer the war's threat to Australia and the more closely it was related to territorial invasion, the lower would be the suicide rate.

Data were collected from two sources — suicide rates *(apparently)* from official records and threat from content analyses of two Australian newspapers. Threat was broken down into two variables — aspect (territorial, logistic, and predictions) and theater (Pacific, North African, and European).

The data for the study were intercorrelated separately for each of the variable combinations above. Results showed negative correlations between threat and suicide for each of the nine possible variable combinations. Overall the correlation was $-.52$, which provided considerable support for the main hypothesis. In addition the correlations were stronger the nearer and more territorial the threat. Unfortunately, although the trends were in the predicted direction, O'Malley did not report statistical comparisons of the coefficients. Statements about comparative magnitudes of correlations must be made with care.

The results of this study are intriguing, considering the rather large correlations between newspaper article content and suicide. Unfortunately, these data are quite weak as a test of the causal hypothesis. There are a host of other variables that may have caused the relationship which have nothing to do with the theory. In fact, O'Malley discussed at great length the possibility that these results may simply have reflected changes in reporting of suicide rather than suicide itself. That is, during war when medical personnel were in short supply, the reporting of suicide might have become imprecise. Times of unusual threat may have been accompanied by increased casualties, increased military need for medical personnel, decreased supply of medical personnel for autopsies, and decreased reporting of suicide.

This study illustrates well the problems of drawing causal inferences from correlational data. All this study established was the existence of a relationship between two variables. More data would be necessary to establish causality. A next logical step would be to measure social integration and, using appropriate procedures such as path analysis, test whether threat seems to lead to integration which leads to suicide reduction.

5.0 MULTIPLE-GROUP DESIGNS

This chapter is concerned with the simplest of the experimental designs — the multiple group. These designs can involve comparison of two or more treatment groups that differ along a single independent variable. Included in this chapter are designs involving both single and multiple observations. Multiple-group time series designs are covered, as are ex post facto designs. The single characteristic that was used to assign designs to this particular chapter was the existence of a single independent variable in the design, exclusive of time or measurement period. These designs may include any number of measurements.

Two-Group Design

The simplest experimental design is the two group, which involves two variables — one independent and one dependent. The independent variable represents group membership and has two values or levels although, as will be seen in the next section, there is no reason why independent variables are limited to two values. The dependent variable is the measured characteristic of subjects that is free to take on any value possible. The structure is:

$$X_1 \, O_1$$
$$X_2 \, O_1$$

where the X's represent the two treatment groups and the O's are observations of the dependent variable. The levels of the independent variable might be treatments or conditions created or observed by the experimenter in a laboratory or field setting. In either event the investigator assigns subjects to conditions, ideally at random, and observes or measures levels of the dependent variable.

The major advantage of the two-group design over the nonexperimental designs is the control achieved by randomly assigning subjects to groups. If one can be certain that random assignment was achieved and that the two subject groups were truly equivalent, and if one can be assured that the only common difference in experience by the two groups was the treatment, one can be quite confident that differences in the dependent variable were due to the independent variable. The trick is to be sure that control was exercised over all factors irrelevant to the study. These conditions are not always easy to meet, and many times reinterpretations of studies are made based on the hypothesis that certain confounding variables explained results.

Of particular concern in this design is bias in assignment of subjects to groups since it is not always possible to use a truly random procedure. In some instances subjects must volunteer for treatment, or subjects are members of larger social units which must be assigned intact. This last case often occurs in educational research where treatments are assigned to entire classes. When assignment is made in this way, the true subject of the study is the class and not the individual student. In other words students are nested or contained in classes, and there may well be idiosyncratic class characteristics that produce nonequivalent assignment of students to treatments. Also, with social groups, treatments may affect the groups as a whole and may interact with group dynamics. Thus effects found for one group of people may not generalize to another, and the response of a particular person may vary depending upon other people in the group. Procedures are available for handling this problem and will be discussed later.

When subjects are not randomly assigned, it is often difficult to draw definitive conclusions from a study. When random assignment is impossible, there are two approaches, admittedly patchwork, that may add some confidence to the conclusions. The first involves checking for initial equivalence of groups, and the second involves selecting matched cases from all those available. With both approaches the variables used for matching are characteristics of the subjects or, ideally, a pretest on the dependent variable. The testing for pretest equivalence is a common procedure even with random assignment. When pretest differences are found, conclusions must be made with extreme care. The matching procedure, or ex post facto design, will be discussed in a later section of this monograph.

Nonrandom subject loss is another potential problem with the two-group design. Bias in subject loss can be as damaging as in subject assignment, as it destroys the entire concept of randomness. Subject loss is especially problematic in studies where the time between subject assignment to conditions and measurement of the dependent variable is long, or where treatments are of such a nature that subjects do not complete them. Studies involving some treatments that are unpleasant or painful may result in systematic subject attrition. In the psychotherapy research area, sometimes treatment groups consist of those individuals who completed treatment, compared with control subjects. There is an obvious bias in such studies since dropout or noncompletion of treatment is not a random event.

Other sources of invalidity are of no more concern to the two-group study than to other studies, and points made previously about them are relevant here. Overall, the advantage of the two-group study is its ability to control treatments so that only levels of the independent variable of interest are compared. However, independent variables are often complex situations which can differ along many dimensions. A well-designed study is based on a careful and thorough analysis of these dimensions and assures that the treatment conditions created truly reflect the underlying theory or hypothesis.

The analysis of data in the two-group study usually involves comparing group means on the dependent variables of interest. This can be done with a simple t test or with the analysis of variance (ANOVA). The results are equivalent with either approach. The analysis of variance will be discussed in greater detail in the next section.

There is one distinction that needs to be made here and that concerns the level of measurement of the independent variable. The underlying characteristic upon which the group membership variable is based may be discrete, such as sex or race, or it may be continuous, such as dosage of drug or amount of time spent in an activity. With the discrete variable, the numbers represent convenient labels, and intermediate values are meaningless, except, perhaps, as additional labels. Thus with the sex variable if males are considered to have a value of 1, and females a value of 2, a value for sex of 1.5 has no meaning in relationship to males and females. However, with continuous variables, such as time, 1.5 minutes has meaning in relationship to 1 and 2 minutes; it is the midpoint between them. With a continuous independent variable, one can state a functional relationship between it and the dependent variable, and one can interpolate to values between those chosen for study. For example, if one were to find that a student can learn twice as much material in 4 hours than 2 hours, one might interpolate that one and one-half as much material is learned in 3 hours than in 2 hours.

If the independent variable is discrete or if one is not going to extend conclusions to values of the independent variable that were not included in the study, the independent variable is said to be a *fixed effect*. On the other hand if the underlying continuum of the independent variable is continuous, and if conclusions are made to values not in the design, the independent variable is said to be a *random effect*. One should note that when an independent variable is truly discrete, one cannot extend conclusions to other values of the variable and in fact intermediate values might not exist. Therefore, the effect must be fixed. When the independent variable is continuous, one can choose whether to treat the effect as fixed or random. For example, suppose one designs a study to determine the effects on voter preference for a particular condidate of two media presentations, one lasting for one minute and the other lasting for five minutes. If one were to find that the five-minute spot was more effective than the one-minute spot at inducing a favorable response toward the candidate, one could treat the effect as fixed or random. If fixed, one would conclude that the five-minute presentation was more effective than the shorter one, but one would make no statements about the effects of presentation length in general. That is, one would not conclude that a two-minute presentation would be more effective than a one, or a three-minute one better than a two. If this were done, the effect would be random, as one would be interpolating results to intermediate values not chosen for study.

In the social sciences, independent variables are usually considered fixed, especially when there are only two levels. It is not particularly good practice to choose only two levels for a random variable since only two of many possible points are included along the measurement continuum, and the actual form of the relationship between independent and dependent variables will be based on too little information.

With fixed variables or effects, one can select levels to compare two procedures, treatments, or conditions or to compare one treatment to a control of no treatment. In many cases this distinction is somewhat arbitrary as control conditions may actually involve treatment, but perhaps not conducted by the researcher. A good example is in the area of psychotherapy research where a particular treatment approach might be compared to no treatment. The most common practice is to compare individuals who receive treatment, for example systematic desensitization, to individuals who spend an equivalent amount of time on a waiting list. However, it is difficult to say that the control subjects receive no treatment — only that they receive no professional treatment. They may in fact receive help from family and friends, which is indeed a treatment. What is compared in these studies is professional treatment and naturally occurring treatment in the community.

Laboratory research certainly provides more control over alternative treatments for control group subjects. However, even in highly controlled settings, the control subjects experience something during the time they are in the control condition. This control treatment is carefully chosen to be neutral and may involve giving the subjects some task or activity to occupy their time. Elements of this control activity are designed carefully to control various aspects of actual treatment. In verbal learning experiments it is common to give control subjects a mental task to prevent them from mentally rehearsing material, and in studies involving manual or perceptual tasks, control tasks might hold fatigue constant.

Although with fixed effects one does not extend conclusions to intermediate values of the independent variable, there is always some interpretation or generalization beyond the exact conditions of the study. That is, one interprets how far the experimental conditions can be extended. In a psychotherapy study, one decides whether results can generalize to the particular treatment approach applied by different therapists, at different institutions, and with different orientations. Unfortunately, treatments sharing the same label are not necessarily equivalent. Generalization is a difficult task requiring much judgment and knowledge of a content area. Replication is important for testing the same hypothesis utilizing somewhat different operationalizations of the independent variable and instruments for the dependent variable.

Multiple-Group Posttest Design

An expansion of the two-group design is the multiple-group design, with a single dependent variable measured once and an independent variable that can have any number of values or levels. This design has the structure:

$$X_1 \; O_1$$
$$X_2 \; O_1$$
$$\cdot \qquad \cdot$$
$$\cdot \qquad \cdot$$
$$\cdot \qquad \cdot$$
$$X_n \; O_1$$

For the most part all of the discussion related to the advantages and problems of the two group study applies to the multiple group. The multiple group has the additional advantage that more levels of the independent variable can be compared, and more control groups can be included. For example, if one were to try out a new procedure of some sort, one might compare the new procedure or treatment against both no treatment and a commonly used treatment. This would represent a double control in that one would establish that the conventional procedure worked better than no procedure in a particular setting and that the new procedure was better or worse than the conventional.

In the previous section I made the distinction between fixed and random effects. One can have fixed effects with any number of groups, as some variables may be represented by many possible discrete values. Occupation, for example, may be categorized into hundreds of levels, although this would not be practical in a real design. Random effects become useful when there are several values of the independent variable. For example, one might conduct a study to ascertain the effects of varying doses of a particular drug on memory. The effects of five doses of the drug could be measured on the number of items remembered after a single presentation of a word list. Since the independent variable would be random, one could determine a mathematical function relating dosage to memory.

The major data-analytic tool for such multiple-group studies is the analysis of variance. This procedure is designed to statistically compare two or more treatment groups on the dependent variable. The mechanics involve a comparison of two variances derived from the data. The first is the between-group variance, that is, the variance of the treatment means between or among groups. The second is the within-group variance or the variance among subjects within each treatment group. If there are no group differences other than those resulting by chance, variance between groups should be equivalent to variance within groups. That is, the two variances would be equivalent statistically or there would be no significant group differences. If there are group differences, there should be more between-group variance than within-group variance, and the comparison should become statistically significant. This discussion is admittedly an oversimplification of ANOVA; the interested reader should consult a text on statistics for computational details (e.g., Iversen and Norpoth, 1976; Myers, 1972; Winer, 1971).

Multiple-Group Pretest-Posttest Design

By adding pretest observations of the dependent variable to the first two designs of this chapter, one will create a pretest-posttest design as diagramed below:

$$O_1 \ X_1 \ O_2$$

$$O_1 \ X_2 \ O_2$$

$$\cdot \qquad \cdot \qquad \cdot$$

$$\cdot \qquad \cdot \qquad \cdot$$

$$\cdot \qquad \cdot \qquad \cdot$$

$$O_1 \ X_n \ O_2$$

The advantage of this design lies in being able to demonstrate the level of the dependent variable before as well as after treatment. This can be useful information for establishing that groups were initially equivalent and for providing a baseline against which to compare treatment effects, of particular value when a control group is not available.

Pretest-posttest designs are especially popular in program evaluation studies where the research question concerns the efficacy of programs or specific interventions for producing change in participants. Many of these studies may not have available an untreated control, as all people available as subjects may receive some treatment or intervention. This is especially true in educational, mental health, and social service program research.

It is always preferable to have proper control groups, and, as with the one-group pretest-posttest, the existence of change with the current design does not indicate the factors that caused it. If a nontreated control group is unavailable in a study which compared two types of interventions, one would never be certain what might have happened to subjects in either treatment group had they received no treatment. The use of pretests is not a good substitute for proper control groups.

The addition of pretests to a design creates the potential for instrument reactivity with treatments. As discussed in the previous chapter, subjects may be affected by pretests in such a manner as to influence their reactions to the treatments. Perhaps the best control for this possibility is that used in the Solomon four-group design, described in the next chapter.

Other problems with this design are similar to those of the previous two in this chapter. However, there does exist a particular problem in the analysis and interpretation of change data generated in pretest-posttest studies. One possible means of analyzing these data would be to compare groups on average changes from pre- to posttesting, subtracting posttest from pretest scores, but there is a significant problem with the use of change scores and that involves measurement error.

It is widely known that the reliability of the difference between two imperfect measures is worse than the reliability of either measure itself. Suppose one were to administer an attitude questionnaire to a group of subjects before and after an attitude change treatment. Furthermore, suppose the instrument had a reliability of .90, a very good reliability coefficient for such a measure. Unless scores on the pretest were uncorrelated with scores on the posttest, a very unlikely phenomenon, the reliability of the difference scores would be less than .90. In fact if the correlation between scores at the two times was .70, the reliability of the difference would be only .67, based on the formula provided by Guilford (1954: 394). Difference scores based on less reliable instruments would have considerably worse reliability.

A second problem with pretest-posttest data involves a statistical artifact, regression toward the mean. This artifact is an outcome of measurement error that accompanies imperfectly reliable instruments. It is a statistical fact that scores on an instrument for subjects extreme in value relative to all people who might be measured tend to become less extreme upon retesting. If an individual has a score that is unusually high, it probably is associated with a large error component. It is unlikely that, upon retesting, that individual will score as high again. Thus scores of individuals tend to become closer to the average score upon retesting. This tendency is greater the further away from the mean the initial score.

When a group of subjects produces scores that are extreme, chances are that part of that extreme score was due to random error; and upon retesting, even with no intervention, the scores will fall toward the mean, and the gorup will seem to demonstrate change. If two groups were each tested twice on the same instrument and one happened to be more extreme than the other, one would expect the more extreme group to show more change than the less extreme group merely as a function of regression toward the mean. If different treatments were applied to the groups, it might be difficult to separate real treatment effects from regression toward the mean.

These problems have led some to question whether change scores are at all valuable in research studies (Cronbach and Furby, 1970). In fact if random assignment occurs and subjects are initially equivalent, comparison of posttest scores alone will indicate if the dependent variable differed among levels of the independent variable. If random assignment did not occur, statistical procedures are at best a weak means of patching the design. (For a discussion of the problems and procedures for the measurement of change see Harris, 1963.)

Two procedures for analyzing data from pretest-posttest designs have already been discussed. The analysis of change scores directly is relatively simple and easy to interpret. Unfortunately, it suffers from the problems of low reliability and statistical artifacts. The second procedure that has been suggested is to use the pretest scores merely to verify that the groups were initially equivalent and then to test for posttest differences. That is, if all groups show pretest equivalence, differential scores upon posttesting would indicate differential change. Of course if pretest differences were found, posttests would not indicate change. A problem with this approach is best illustrated with an example. Suppose one were to collect both pretest and posttest data for two groups. Considering the sample sizes and variance of both groups, suppose it would take a mean difference between groups of exactly 5.00 to achieve significance. If one were to find for pretests that the difference between means was 4.99, one would conclude no pretest differences. Now suppose for posttest the difference was 5.00. It would be quite difficult to argue that there was differential change between groups because the pretest was not significant but the posttest was. One must be quite cautious in drawing conclusions with such procedures.

Other procedures for analyzing these data have been developed. ANOVA can be used for this design and is quite reasonable if there has been random assignment to treatment conditions. Analysis of covariance has been suggested where posttests are compared after being statistically adjusted for pretest scores. This procedure can provide a more sensitive test than analysis of posttests alone, but it is a poor substitute for random assignment.

Ex Post Facto Design

The ex post facto design is a patchwork procedure intended to make a pseudo-experimental design out of a nonexperimental one. This is done in observational studies where one variable can be identified as independent or in experimental designs where it was not possible to randomly assign subjects. The logic of the design, as mentioned previously, is to match on several critical variables subjects in two or more groups and then to analyze data from the matched subjects only. The design is diagramed as:

$$X_1 \ O_1 \ \text{Match}$$
$$X_2 \ O_1$$

where the two groups are matched after treatment.

For example, suppose a study is designed to ascertain if job enlargement leads to less absenteeism than traditional work design. One might find a factory whose management agrees to participate in an enlargement experiment. However, management might insist that employees be given a choice whether they want to try the new system or stick with the old, traditional assembly line process. One could assign the volunteers to enlargement and nonvolunteers to the control group and then check absenteeism for the two groups. Since random assignment would not occur, one would not be certain that enlargement was the cause of absenteeism differences. One could therefore select samples for analysis that would be matched on variables considered to be relevant. In this example one might match on salary, tenure, age, sex, marital status, history of serious medical problems, and job performance. One would then have two samples that were equivalent on at least these seven variables.

Unfortunately, the two groups would still differ on one important variable — volunteering. It may well be that those who volunteered would respond favorably and show absenteeism improvement. The nonvolunteers might well react in the opposite way, and if enlargement were instituted throughout the company, the net result might be no difference in average absenteeism, although some employees might improve and some become worse. In the final analysis one cannot match for every possible variable, and one can never know for certain which variables are most crucial.

Another major problem with matching is shrinkage in sample size with multiple matching variables. Campbell and Stanley (1963; 70) illustrate well this problem citing a study conducted by Chapin (1955). They point out that Chapin's original sample of 1194 shrunk to only 46 after matching. This shrinkage alone caused severe problems for generalization. Also, they note that the original effects found with the entire sample shrunk considerably after matching and question whether they might have totally disappeared had other matching variables been added.

Nevertheless, the ex post facto design may be an improvement over the two-group design with no random assignment, although without random assignment the design is hardly experimental. Perhaps the most crucial variable for matching would be a pretest on the dependent variable itself. This at least would enable the investigator to state that the groups were equivalent initially on this variable. Conclusions could then be drawn about differntial change, although its cause still might be the selection process interacting with treatment. In the enlargement example, even if employees were matched for prior absenteeism, the only firm conclusion would be that job enlargement may reduce absenteeism for employees willing to volunteer for it. Its efficacy with non-volunteers would be a question for empirical verification.

Multiple-Group Time Series Design

The final design to be covered in this chapter is the multiple-group time series. This design involves multiple measurements of the dependent variable on two or more groups representing levels of the independent variable. It is an extension of the pretest-posttest design where there are more than two measurement periods and an extension of the interrupted time series to multiple groups. It is represented as:

$$O_1 \ O_2 \ O_3 \ X_1 \ O_4 \ O_5 \ O_6$$

$$O_1 \ O_2 \ O_3 \ X_2 \ O_4 \ O_5 \ O_6$$

for a two-group, six-measurement design.

As with the time series design for one group, the multiple-group time series can involve a few measurements over a relatively brief duration or many measurements taken over considerable time. The number of measurements determines the type of analysis to be used, as some analyses are not feasible for many testings, while others cannot be used if there are not a sufficient number of time periods selected. Some of these procedures assume that time periods between measurements are constant, although designs for which ANOVA would be appropriate can have unequal periods.

The simplest time series design is one where there are two or more levels of an independent variable, and these treatments are applied in the middle of a series of observations of the dependent variable. The advantages and problems with this design are similar to the pretest-posttest discussed earlier in this chapter. This particular design is potentially more sensitive to instrument reactivity due to the repeated application of the instrument, although subjects may tend to adapt to being measured. An advantage of this design is that it allows determination of trends on the dependent variable before and after treatment. Before treatment this would indicate whether the dependent variable was stable over time for all treatment groups. This is especially important when subjects are not randomly assigned. After treatment the multiple measurements indicate whether treatment effects occur immediately or last for an extended period of time. Program evaluations often take relatively long-range measurements on subjects to see if gains made as the result of a program or intervention sustain themselves over time. Such follow-up studies are frequent in mental health and criminal justice.

With time series involving several measurement periods, the analysis of variance can be used to test for differential change or trends among treatment groups. However, with several measurements, the analysis of variance suffers the problem of autocorrelation. That is, with repeated measurements, those measurements occurring more closely to one another in time tend to be more highly correlated than those occurring more distally. This results in biased statistical tests and may indicate false statistical significance. Adjustments are possible, although they may not be totally satisfactory. An alternative approach would be to use the multivariate analysis of variance (MANOVA), which does not suffer from autocorrelation. Discussion of this procedure would be beyond the present scope. The interested reader is referred to Cole and Grizzle (1966) or Poor (1973).

For many measurements, neither ANOVA nor MANOVA would be possible. If there are 50 or more measurements, ARIMA can be used. These applications are discussed by Glass, Willson, and Gottman (1975: Chapter 8) and by Chatfield (1975).

Examples

Two-Group Design. Experimental designs in field settings are rather rare due to problems involved in gaining control over subject assignment and confounding factors. An exception is a study by Waldo and Chiricos (1977), who were able to randomly assign prison inmates to one of two treatments which they did not create. Since there was in fact random assignment, this design is experimental.

The question of interest in this study was whether work release is effective in reducing recidivism among prison inmates. The investigators were able to assign at random prisoners to either work release or traditional treatment. As a check on random assignment, the two groups were compared on several characteristics, particularly those related to prior arrest record. No significant differences were found, which gave the investigators greater confidence in their results.

Measures of recidivism were taken for each subject in the study. Since the investigators were unable to select a single measure, they included 18, each of which was analyzed separately. There were no statistically significant differences found between the two groups on any of the recidivism measures. Thus work release, which is widely assumed to be effective in reducing recidivism, was found to be no better than more traditional treatment.

It is difficult to find fault with the design of this study since subjects were randomly assigned to both the experimental and control groups. One might wish to investigate further what the control subjects received in the way of treatment, as other possible control treatments might yield different results. The question here is whether the control treatment used can generalize to other prison systems. This question can also be raised concerning the generalizability of the sample. That is, would these results be found in other facilities with different inmate populations or different operating environments? Such questions suggest the need for replication of studies, especially by other investigators in other geographic areas. Replication is an essential element in verifying hypotheses.

Multigroup Design. Reilly, Tenopyr, and Sperling (1979) conducted a study to determine the effects of job previews on job acceptance and survival of applicants to a telephone company. A total of 325 job applicants were randomly assigned to one of three conditions which varied only on the type of preview given. In the first or realistic condition, applicants were given balanced information, some favorable and some unfavorable, about working for the company. The second was the favorable condition in which only favorable information was given. The third condition was a control that was given no additional information. There were four separate dependent variables separately analyzed in the study by means of chi-square statistics appropriate for frequency data. Only the results of the job acceptance variable will be summarized here.

Job acceptance rates were found to differ significantly among the treatment groups (acceptance rate = 56.1%, 68.6%, and 71.6% for realistic, favorable, and control, respectively). Subsequent analysis indicated that this difference was accounted for solely by the lower acceptance rate for the realistic preview group.

These data suggest that the realistic preview reduced the frequency of acceptance for those job applicants receiving it. Since the design was experimental, one would assume that the only systematic difference among groups was the independent variable. This yielded conclusions quite strongly that the preview led to decreased acceptance. That is, this study can be considered internally valid. However, external validity or generalization to other samples might be more problematic. This particular study was done with telephone operator candidates at one particular compnay. It is an empirical question whether these results would be found in another organization with different personnel procedures and with another population applying for different types of jobs. For definitive conclusions that could be widely generalized, this study would have to be replicated at additional organizations and for additional job categories.

Two-Group Multiple-Measures Design. Stephens and Burroughs (1978) conducted a study to ascertain whether different operant conditioning procedures would be effective in reducing employee absenteeism in a hospital. They created two treatment conditions as the independent variable and measured absenteeism three times. The two treatment conditions were slight variations of a lottery in which employees who met the criteria of good attendance would be eligible for a cash prize in a drawing. One condition required no absenteeism during a three-week period while the other required attendance on eight secret, random days during the same three weeks. Data on absenteeism were collected for both treatment groups during three time periods — before, during, and after treatment.

The results of this study are depicted in Figure 5.1. As can be seen, there were small and nonsignificant differences between the two treatment groups. Likewise, there was a nonsignificant interaction between treatments and repeated measures, indicating similar effects for both groups. However, there was a strong retesting effect with absenteeism declining during the lottery period and increasing after its termination to a level higher than before treatment.

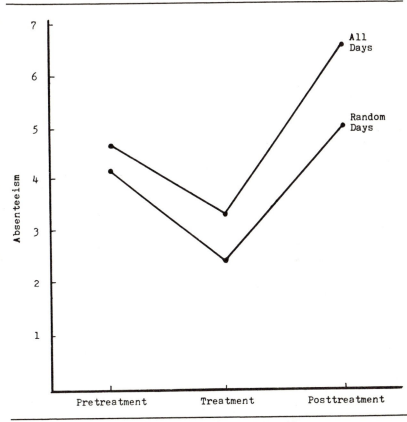

Figure 5.1 Absenteeism as a Function of Experimental Condition

Although this study is experimental, it is inconclusive due to the investigators' choice of independent variable levels. While it provides strong evidence that both treatments were equal in their effects, there was no control group that received neither procedure. In effect each treatment group served as its own control through the repeated measurement, but there was no control for history apparently because the investigators felt that there were no other events that occurred which might have confounded the results.

Perhaps more important, considering that this was an organizational field study, is the potential for Hawthorne effects. That is, the effectiveness of these procedures might have been due to the subjects' knowledge that they were in an experiment. What suggests that there might be a transitory effect was the absenteeism increase during the final phase of the study after treatment was discontinued. This might have reflected the employees' putting off discretionary absences until after the lottery. These results certainly suggest the need for a longer term study to determine if the absenteeism reduction would continue over an extended period.

This study points out the limitations of even an experimental design, especially in field settings. Despite that fact that it was rather well-designed and implemented, it was still not conclusive. This is because it allowed only comparison of the two treatment conditions, which do not necessarily represent all reasonable treatment conditions possible. Furthermore, there is the possibility of Hawthorne effects which were not controlled. Finally, as with most studies, there is the generalizability problem, and one cannot be certain that the same results would be found with a different organization or other employees.

6.0 FACTORIAL DESIGNS

To this point the designs discussed involved only a single independent plus a retesting variable. However, most experimental designs encountered in practice have several independent variables and are meant to determine their combined effects on the dependent variable in question. Usually the independent variables are placed into a factorial structure for ease of analysis. These structures can be simple or complex, depending upon the number and nature of variables chosen. It is the purpose of this chapter to review factorial designs, from the most simple involving two independent variables to the complex involving several.

Two × Two Factorial Design

By far the simplest factorial design is the 2 × 2, which consists of two independent variables, each taking on two levels or values. The design is structured so that every level of one independent variable is crossed or associated with every level of the other. For example if the independent variables are sex (male vs. female) and treatment (A vs. B), the design would consist of four treatment combinations or cells — males receiving treatment A, males receiving treatment B, females receiving A, and

TABLE 6.1 Example of a 2 × 2 Factorial Design

Treatment	Sex	
	Male	Female
A	Subject 1	Subject 11
	Subject 2	Subject 12
	Subject 3	Subject 13
	Subject 4	Subject 14
	Subject 5	Subject 15
B	Subject 6	Subject 16
	Subject 7	Subject 17
	Subject 8	Subject 18
	Subject 9	Subject 19
	Subject 10	Subject 20

females receiving B. The design structure is outlined in Table 6.1 for a study with 20 subjects, 5 per cell. As can be seen, every possible combination of independent variable levels is represented, and each cell contains the same number of subjects who are different individuals or social entities. These last two conditions are not necessary, but they greatly simplify the analysis.

For the most part the advantages and problems with the factorial design are similar to those of the multigroup. However, the factorial design allows the addition of variables which may be used as controls for confounding factors or as additional aspects to be studied. An example of additional control is the Solomon four-group design, discussed in the following section, which has as one independent variable whether the subject receives a pretest. This design allows a determination of instrument reactivity.

Most factorial studies contain independent variables that are factors of interest rather than possible confounds such as instrument reactivity. These designs have the advantage that they allow determination of joint effects of independent variables in addition to their independent effects. These are represented as interactions and main effects, respectively.

A main effect in a factorial design is the independent (in a conceptual rather than mathematical sense) effect of a particular variable. In the previous example there would be a main effect for sex and a main effect for treatment. Each would involve a comparison of all subjects at each of its two levels. One would compare all males with all females on the dependent measure, regardless of their level of treatment. Likewise, the treatment main effect would involve a comparison of all A subjects with all B subjects, regardless of their sex. This is done by ignoring the other variable and *collapsing* across it. Means would be calculated for all males and all females by collapsing across the levels of the treatment variable. The same would be done with sex for the treatment variable.

The interaction is the joint or qualified effect taking into account both variables. The interaction in the example would be concerned with whether differences between treatment A and B were the same for males and females, whether there were main effects. In other words, if females are higher on the dependent measure for B than A, do males show the same pattern? The same pattern can exist even though the means for males may be higher or lower than for females.

Interaction can best be understood by illustration. Figure 6.1 indicates graphically several possible combinations of main effects and interactions. For each graph the x-axis represents the independent variable, treatment, which takes on its two values, A and B. The y-axis represents the dependent variable, and the sex variable is represented by the two lines, labelled male and female.

Figure 6.1a indicates two main effects and no interaction. Females are higher than males for both treatments, and treatment B is higher than treatment A for both sexes. There is no interaction since the pattern of results is the same for both sexes. This is reflected by the fact that the two lines are parallel.

Figure 6.1b indicates a case of interaction with no main effects. The pattern for males and females is exactly opposite. Males are higher on A than B, and females are higher on B than A. Overall neither treatment is higher than the other, and neither sex is higher than the other. The interaction is indicated by the 'x' pattern formed by the two lines.

Figures 6.1c and 6.1d illustrate two other possible interactions. In c there is no difference on the treatment variable for males, but there is for females. Furthermore, females and males do not differ on A, only on B. In 6.1d females are higher than males on both treatments but show an opposite pattern. Where females are higher on B than A, males are higher on A than B. This pattern is similar to 6.1b except that there is now a sex main effect.

Interactions are more precise statements of the results than main effects and usually once an interaction is found, the main effects should be discarded. This is especially true with patterns like 6.1c where a difference is only found for females. To say there is a treatment main effect, though technically correct, implies that all subjects, on the average, are different at one treatment than the other, a situation that is not true since only females show the effect.

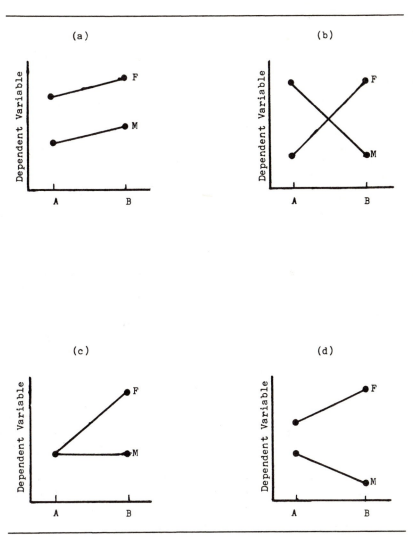

Figure 6.1 Examples of Possible Interactions for a 2 × 2 Design

The analysis of factorial data is conducted with the analysis of variance. As mentioned in the last chapter, ANOVA involves calculating two variance estimates and testing them for statistical significance. With the more complex 2 × 2 design, however, there are three effects to test, not one. Therefore, in addition to an estimate of within-group or error variance, one must devise an estimate for all three between-group effects — the two mains and interaction. Total between group variance can be partitioned into components for each of the effects to be tested. Each is compared to error variance using the same statistical logic discussed in the previous chapter. Thus there would be three tests conducted with the possibility that any or all are significant.

Earlier mention was made of two limiting assumptions that simplified ANOVA; first, that different subjects were in each cell of the design and, second, that there were the same number of subjects in each cell. Having different subjects in each cell makes this a *between-subjects* design, which is the easiest to analyze. However, it is not necessary to have all between-subjects effects, and the same subjects can be found in more than one cell making the effect *within subject*. The most common circumstance in which this occurs is with the pretest-posttest design. One of the independent variables is the time of measurement which is included as a within-subject effect in the ANOVA. With such a design the treatment main effect indicates that ignoring or combining retestings, one treatment is higher on the dependent variable than the other. The main effect for retesting indicates that average posttests differ from average pretests. The interaction indicates that the two treatments differed in the pattern of scores from pretest to posttest. This is the effect that indicates group differences, usually the question of primary interest.

The within-subject variable is not limited to retesting, and in fact multiple levels of a treatment variable can be applied to the same subjects. In the Sex × Treatment example, both treatments could be given to each subject. The advantage is that this tends to reduce error variance due to idiosyncratic differences among subjects. At the same time it creates the problem that treatments are confounded with order of presentation and with retesting. Order can be controlled with a procedure termed *counterbalancing*. That is, half the subjects receive A first and half receive B first, allowing one to compare the same treatments given at each order. However, this procedure confounds exposure to prior treatments with number of measurements, making it difficult to separate instrument reactivity from treatment carryover. Procedures to control for reactivity are discussed below and could be incorporated with counterbalancing. It is always hoped that there will not be order effects, because such effects complicate interpretation of results.

Another complication arises in a factorial design when cell sizes are not equal. With equal sample sizes or *orthogonal designs,* the independent variables are totally independent or uncorrelated. As sample sizes become unequal, the independent variables become dependent and correlated (nonorthogonal). Hence it is difficult to determine the inde-

TABLE 6.2   Examples of Equal and Nonequal Sample Size Factorial
Designs

(a)

| | A | | |
B	a_1	a_2	Total
b_1	M = 100 n = 50	M = 150 n = 50	M = 125 n = 100
b_2	M = 200 n = 50	M = 250 n = 50	M = 225 n = 100
Total	M = 150 n = 100	M = 200 n = 100	

(b)

| | A | | |
B	a_1	a_2	Total
b_1	M = 100 n = 10	M = 150 n = 90	M = 145 n = 100
b_2	M = 200 n = 90	M = 250 n = 10	M = 205 n = 100
Total	M = 190 n = 100	M = 160 n = 100	

pendent effects of each independent variable since they are confounded
with one another. Table 6.2 shows what inequality of cell sizes does to
main effect means. In both designs shown, the individual cell means and
total number of subjects are identical. However, the main effect or
marginal means are different due to the unequal sample sizes. In fact the
means for treatment A completely reversed from a_2 being larger than a_1
to a_2 being smaller. Statistical tests for significant differences between
these means will be distorted in the same way. Hence, straightforward
ANOVA might not yield correct conclusions. The solution to this problem is complex and certainly beyond the scope of this discussion. Proper
procedures for analyzing such data are discussed in other sources (Spector, 1980; Spector, Voissem, and Cone, forthcoming).

Solomon Four-Group Design

The Solomon four-group design is a combination of the 2×2 factorial and the pretest-posttest, used to control for instrument reactivity. This design is similar to factorial designs because subjects are placed into a 2×2 structure and similar to the pretest-posttest because subjects receive two measurements, but in this case only half the subjects receive the pretest. It is represented as:

$$O_1 \; X_1 \; O_2$$

$$X_1 \; O_2$$

$$O_1 \; X_2 \; O_2$$

$$X_2 \; O_2$$

The Solomon four-group design offers all the advantages of the factorial with the additional feature that it tests for instrument reactivity. That is, for both groups one is able to compare subjects who differ only in that they received the pretest. Furthermore, one is able to assess the degree of change that occurred between pretesting and posttesting for each treatment. This design is quite powerful and sees too little application in the social sciences — surprising since it would require little additional effort in many situations.

The basic logic of the Solomon four group could be extended to both larger and smaller designs. For the single-group pretest-posttest, this procedure could be used to control for instrument reactivity by omitting pretests for half the subjects. It could also be used in studies involving more than two groups, using the same idea of adding pretests for half the subjects. The only limitation would be that a sufficient number of subjects must be available for each of the groups in the study.

The analysis of four-group design data is somewhat more complex than analyses discussed earlier. Since only half the subjects receive pretests, the design is incomplete from a statistical perspective. That is, if one were to set all data into an ANOVA design, there would be missing data for half the subjects. Perhaps the best procedure would be to conduct the analysis in stages. The first stage might be to compare the two treatment groups on pretests to verify that there were no pretest differences. This would be a check on random assignment to conditions. If differences exist, it would be difficult to draw definitive conclusions from the study. The second stage would involve an analysis of all posttest scores. These data would fit a 2 × 2 factorial design with treatment level as one factor and pretest (present or absent) as the other. One could then test for treatment differences, the major hypothesis of interest, and instrument reactivity in two ways. First, one would see whether there were significant differences overall between subjects receiving pretests and subjects not receiving pretests. If this test was significant, pretests would be affecting either posttest measurement or treatments. The interaction term would yield a test for a differential effect of pretesting on the two treatments. That is, pretests might affect one treatment more than another, especially if one is a control group that receives no manipulation.

Finally, if there are no pretest differences and no instrument reactivity effects, one might wish either to analyze change scores or to conduct an analysis of posttests adjusted for pretests for those subjects who received pretests. Of course one must take appropriate care in analyzing such data in light of the problems, discussed previously, with change score analysis.

M × N Factorial Design

The 2 × 2 factorial design can be expanded where the independent variables have any number of levels within practical limits. Such designs are an extension of the 2 × 2 and share the same advantages and problems. However, they enable the researcher to investigate more than two levels of the independent variables at one time, often a useful feature.

In designing factorial studies, one must decide how many levels of the independent variable to construct. For some variables, such as sex, there are a limited and fixed number of levels possible. For others the number of possible levels might be unlimited. This is especially true when an independent variable can be represented on a continuous scale, such as time, number of trials, or scores on a test. Such variables are usually treated as fixed, although they could be treated as random. In the social sciences it is rare to find analyses of variance conducted with other than fixed effects.

When independent variables are continuous, and the investigator is not faced with choosing several from all possible levels, it is better to retain the variable's continuous nature than force it into a limited number of categories. This is a procedure often overlooked when the independent variables are characteristics of subjects such as age, income, or scores on psychological tests. In the latter case it is common to dichotomize scores into upper and lower halves, assigning all subjects above the median to one level of the independent variable and subjects with scores below the median to the other. This practice is wasteful in that it ignores the fact that the independent variable was measured with far greater precision than reflected by a two-value variable. The reason for the popularity of such practices can be found in the common preference for certain experimental designs and the analysis of variance.

The same hypotheses can be tested utilizing all the precision in the variables by using multiple regression instead of ANOVA. As discussed previously, multiple regression is a procedure that allows one to specify a linear functional relationship between the dependent variable and the independent variables. An equation is generated of the form:

$$Y = b_O + b_1 x_1 + b_2 x_2 + \ldots + b_n x_n$$

where Y is the dependent variable, the x's are the independent variables, and the b's are constants derived from the data. The mathematical procedures to solve for the constants can be found in many sources including Cohen and Cohen (1975), Kerlinger and Pedhauzer (1973), and Lewis-Beck (1980).

The use of multiple regression for the factorial design enables one to ascertain which main effects and interactions are significantly related to the dependent variable. With continuous independent variables, main effects would be created by entering into the analysis, observations of the independent variables as x values. Interactions would be represented as products of the independent variables. For example, the interaction of variables A and B would be created by multiplying individual scores on A and B (Lewis-Beck, 1980). Since most variables are based on different underlying metrics, it is common to convert both variables to standard scores before multiplying them together.

One complication with using multiple regression in this way is that the effects in the equation may not be independent. That is, the independent variables might be correlated. When this occurs one must take care in interpreting the results. One method for analyzing correlated terms involves stepwise addition or deletion of effects in the analysis. For example, with the stepwise addition procedure, one would first calculate the regression of the dependent variable on the first independent variable. One would then see if adding the second independent variable to the analysis results in a significant increase in relationship between the dependent variable and the two independents. If it does, the next independent variable would be added, and so on until all independent variables are added or until a point is reached at which adding more variables adds nothing to the analysis. Of coures, the major problem with this procedure is specifying the order of entry of the variables, rendering it of maximum value when one has a hypothetical model that specifies order. See Cohen and Cohen (1975) or Kerlinger and Pedhauzer (1973) for details on stepwise procedures.

The interaction term in the m × n design is more difficult to handle than in the 2 × 2 since the graphs can represent more complex patterns. Figure 6.2 illustrates some possible patterns with a 3 × 4 design. Figure 6.2a is a situation in which there are main effects but no interaction. The A variable shows no differences between a_1 and a_2 or between a_3 and a_4, but a difference between each pair. The pattern remains identical for all levels of the B variable, but b_1 is greater than b_2 which is greater than b_3.

Figure 6.2b indicates no main effects but a significant interaction. For b_1 there is an upward trend from a_1 to a_4, while for b_3 the trend is exactly opposite. For b_2 there are no differences among levels of A. Figure 6.2c indicates a complex pattern with all three effects. One should note that the number of possible patterns is far greater than the three shown here, and explanations are more difficult and lengthy than with the 2 × 2 patterns.

Higher Order Factorial Design

Factorial designs are not limited to two independent variables, and higher order designs are frequently encountered. In theory one could include any number of independent variables in a design, provided one could collect data on a sufficient number of subjects. There are, however, practical limitations since the number of subjects is finite, and interpretation of large designs quickly becomes unwieldy.

The advantage of higher order factorials is obvious. One can investigate the combined effects of several independent variables simultaneously. Some variables could be included to control for confounding, such as in the Solomon four-group design. The major disadvantage is the complexity that comes with size. Even when the number of levels of each independent variable is kept small, the number of cells grows quickly as variables are added. For example, a 2 × 2 design has only 4 cells, but a 2 × 2 × 2 × 2 has 16, requiring four times as many subjects. The same four independent variable design with three levels per variable would have 81 cells needing hundreds of subjects to fill.

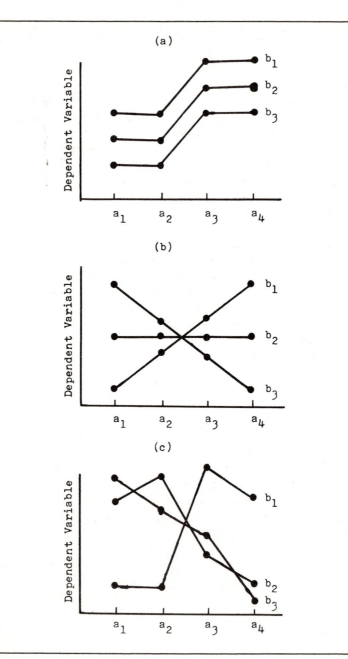

Figure 6.2 Examples of Interactions in m × n Designs

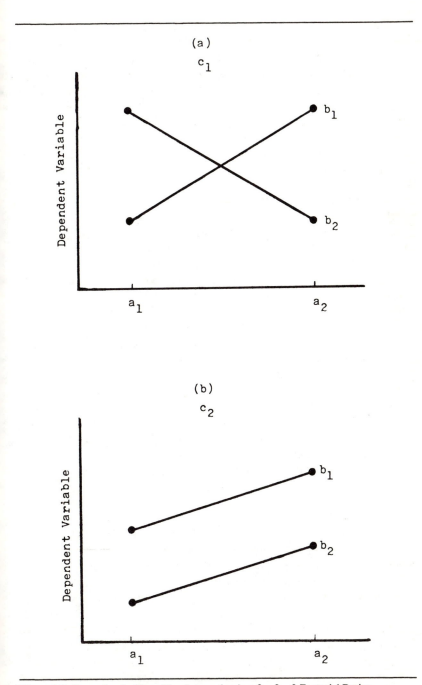

Figure 6.3 Example of a Three-Way Interaction in a $2 \times 2 \times 2$ Factorial Design

The number of effects is also compounded with higher order designs. Each higher order introduces another level of interaction, and these higher order interactions are extremely difficult to interpret. A three-way interaction is illustrated for a three-variable design in Figure 6.3. Since a three-way interaction would take a three-dimensional graph to represent, the common practice is to illustrate it with multiple graphs, one for each level of one independent variable. A $2 \times 2 \times 2$ design is illustrated where a three-way interaction exists. In this case the interaction is manifested by a different pattern within each two-variable graph. In Figure 6.3a there is a clear $A \times B$ interaction, while in Figure 6.3b there is no interaction. Thus the interaction between A and B is dependent upon the level of variable C.

Three-way interactions involving more levels become complex to interpret. More difficult is interpretation of still higher order interactions. In fact most researchers will ignore such interactions and consider their variance components to be error variance.

With the three-way design there are, of course, three main effects, one for each independent variable. There are also three two-way interactions, one for each possible combination of independent variables, that is, $A \times B$, $A \times C$, and $B \times C$, and one three-way interaction. With higher order designs there are still more effects, and for each a variance component must be calculated to test for statistical significance.

Within the higher order designs, it is not necessary that all effects be between subject. That is, one can have any combination of between- and within-subject effects. They require some different computational procedures, but basically any combination is allowable. As with the $m \times n$ design, the most common use of this mixture of effect types is to add pretests to the posttests of a between-subjects factorial design. As with the smaller design, the interactions involving the within-subject factor would indicate change on the between-subjects variables or their interactions.

For example, suppose a study were conducted to test the effects on learning of two types of instruction (lecture and seminar) and two schedules (8 hours per week for 8 weeks and 4 hours per week for 16 weeks). Note that elapsed time is confounded with concentration, but in this case there is no interest in separating them. To conduct this study a pool of subjects is acquired and a dependent measure of knowledge appropriate to the content of the course is developed. A good design for this study would be a $2 \times 2 \times 2$ factorial with instruction and schedule as between-subjects components and a pretest-posttest as the within. The retesting variable is added in order to determine if learning occurred, as reflected by change in performance on the dependent varible from before to after treatment. One could omit the retesting variable and focus only on level of knowledge after treatment, attributing posttest differences to the independent variable. However, it would be unknown whether any real change occurred because the posttest differences might merely have reflected pretest differences. Of course with random assignment to conditions and sufficient sample size, one would assume initial equivalence of groups. Unfortunately, random assignment still will not indicate change. It will only indicate after treatment differences. There might well be posttest differences because some conditions caused a performance decrement while others caused an increase, a possibility testable only with repeated measurements.

One should keep in mind that the purpose of this design is to determine both the separate and joint effects of schedule and instruction type on learning. Of the seven effects in this design, only four offer information relevant to this purpose. The interaction terms involving the between-subjects variables and the retesting variable reflect differential learning among subjects in the various treatment groups. The interaction of Retesting × Instruction Type indicates if subjects learned better with lecture or seminar. Likewise, the interaction of retesting by schedule concerns the differential learning of subjects on the 8-week versus the 16-week schedule. The three-way interaction or Retesting × Instruction Type × Schedule reflects the interactive effects on learning of schedule and instruction type. For example, it might be found that for lecture, the 8-week schedule results in better learning while for seminar neither schedule results in significantly more learning. Thus the effects of each variable are qualified by the other. Although it might be correct based on a significant main effect to conclude that seminar was superior to lecture in student learning, the more precise conclusion would be to refer to the interaction. It might well be that seminar under the 16-week schedule is the best procedure, but the other three do not differ from one another. Thus seminar with an 8-week schedule would be no better than lecture with either schedule and would only show superiority with the longer time span.

One final effect, of particular value when none of the three interaction terms is significant, is the main effect for retesting. This effect indicates change for all groups combined and would show if there was significant learning by all subjects regardless of condition and despite no treatment differences. All treatments might be equally effective or ineffective, a possibility tested with the retesting main effect.

It should be apparent at this point that higher order factorial designs are complex to interpret. Their advantage in allowing joint effects of independent variables to be studied is partially offset by their complexity of analysis and interpretation. These designs remain powerful tools for research when used properly by skilled investigators.

Hierarchical Design

To this point two types of independent variables in factorial designs, the between-subjects and within-subject, have been covered. There is a third, and that is the nested or hierarchical variable. A nested, in contrast to a between-subjects, variable is one in which all levels of the nested variable are not crossed or represented in all levels of other between-subjects variables.

The concept of nesting is not new; in between-subjects designs one can consider subjects to be nested in treatment groups. That is, there are different subjects in each group. This stands in contrast to the within-subject design where each subject is represented at each level of the independent variable. However, effects can also be nested when the levels of an independent variable are found only at some levels of another independent variable. Most often this occurs when subjects are members of preexisting groups or classifications, and entire groups are assigned to treatment conditions. If subjects are not randomly assigned to groups, or if treatments involve interaction among group members, it is the entire group that becomes the subject rather than each member. If many groups exist, one can assign them at random to conditions and still retain features of random assignment to conditions. In many cases conclusions must be made to the group rather than to the individual.

Probably the most common situation where individual subjects are in groups of some sort involves research on students who are nested in classes that are assigned to treatments. In such cases it would be a mistake to analyze the data as if the classes did not exist, because there is a confounding of the treatment with class membership. There might well be, and often is, an interaction between the characteristics of the classes and the treatments. When this is the case, the data are analyzed as if classes are the subjects, although the data from individual class members are still used. Thus in designs where subjects are nested in units which are assigned to treatments, one must have a sufficient number of units available for analysis.

The analysis of hierarchical variables within a factorial design is done with the analysis of variance, which has specific procedures for such situations. Such an analysis is a two-step process where first there is a test for significant differences among groups. If groups are equivalent within treatments, one can analyze the data as if subjects were not tested in them. If there are differences among groups, the group itself is the subject for analysis.

Often one does not purposely design a study to be hierarchical, but finds that subjects happen to be part of larger social units which cannot be split. When this is the case, the larger units should initially be considered as the units of analysis, and the design of the study should include enough of the larger units in case there happen to be group differences. In other cases one is interested in the large social unit, but collects data on individuals in the unit. This might occur in educational studies where units are classes, but measurements are taken on individual students. One should be cautious in such cases that one draws proper conclusions either to individual students or to the aggregate classes. If one were to take a class average and use that as the data for analysis, one could draw conclusions to other classes as a whole, but one may not be able to draw conclusions to individual students (see Langbein and Lichtman, 1978, for a discussion of the aggregate bias that occurs when scores are combined for social units). The hierarchical design deals with both the individual subject and the larger unit.

Hierarchical analyses are not often found in the social science literature, although many studies in which subjects are nested in groups ignore the hierarchical nature of the data. In such cases erroneous conclusions can be reached because it may be the interactive effects of the treatment with the group that was responsible for the significant effect rather than the treatment itself.

Designs with a Concomitant Variable

Social science studies tend to be plagued with large error variance due to the complex nature of social phenomena and the vast heterogeneity of individuals and social units. At least two procedures exist within factorial designs (as well as multigroup experimental designs) to remove or statistically control some of this variance. Both procedures accomplish a similar aim, although they use somewhat different procedures. The first is blocking and the second is analysis of covariance (ANCOVA). Both will be discussed, and some contrasts will be drawn.

In a study there are sometimes variables that can be identified as potentially related to the dependent variable, and which might account for error variance in the design. These additional or *concomitant vari-*

ables can be added to the design and handled in a special way that enables one to draw variance out of the error term in the ANOVA or to adjust the dependent variable for the effects of the additional variable.

The idea of blocking is to use a concomitant variable as an additional independent variable in the analysis. Such designs will often include subjects so that there are an equal number at each level of the concomitant variable and an equal number in each cell of the design. Blocked variables often include sex, intelligence, and scores on various psychological tests.

Blocking often increases the precision of a design by reducing the size of the error variance component in the AVOVA. When it is expected that a particular characteristic of subjects or treatments may affect the study, one can control the effect by assuring that an equal number of subjects will be at each level of the blocking variable. In animal research, for example, it is common to block on litter, so that an equal number of animals from each litter would be assigned to a different condition. Thus if one needs 10 animals for each of 3 conditions, one could acquire 10 litters of 3 animals each and assign at random 1 animal per litter to each condition. Litter would become an effect in the analysis, and could be tested to see if there were significant litter differences. Note that with this design there is only a single subject in each treatment by litter cell of the design, making a test for the interaction impossible.

In human research blocking variables often include sex, intelligence, socioeconomic status, and residence region of the country. With continuous variables such as test scores, one would dichotomize or trichotomize, placing subjects into their appropriate level. The blocking variable, if it is in fact related to the dependent variable, increases the likelihood of finding statistical significance on the independent variables of interest. They are treated the same as any independent variable in a factorial design, although one might not be particularly interested in the significance of the blocking variable.

Analysis of covariance accomplishes the same objective, but does so without compressing the continuous variable into several discrete categories. Thus with test scores one would treat the concomitant variable as a *covariate* in the analysis and adjust the dependent variable for it. Precisely how this is done is beyond the scope of this monograph, but ANCOVA is a statistical means of adjusting for the covariate in a design, and it is based on several assumptions which may or may not hold within a given set of data (Wildt and Ahtola, 1978; Winer, 1971).

The ANCOVA is also used as a means of controlling statistically for confounding factors that were not controlled by the experimental design. For example, suppose one designed a study to determine if one teaching method was superior to another. One might assign a class to each method and then compare knowledge gain of both calsses. Forgetting that this is a hierarchical design, it might be found that the average intelligence scores of students in one class tend to be higher than for students of the other. If these scores were available, the classes could be statistically adjusted to equate for intelligence before comparison. Such adjustments are quite sensitive to violations of assumptions underlying ANCOVA and are not always feasible. Unfortunately, there are no good statistical adjustments for poor designs. Conclusive results from this study would require random assignment of students and classes to teaching methods.

Feldt (1958) has compared the use of blocking and ANCOVA for handling concomitant variables. He contrasted the two by analyzing the same data with each. The concomitant variables were continuous, appropriate for ANCOVA. For blocking they were recoded into varying numbers of categories. His conclusions were that ANCOVA was somewhat more precise, not unexpectedly since it uses all the information in the data, but that its sensitivity to violations of assumptions was a major liability. Thus blocking was recommended as it is simpler to use and understand, and it is far less sensitive to violations of assumptions in actual application.

Multivariate Designs

All of the designs discussed thus far have involved a single dependent variable and are considered to be univariate designs despite the fact that they contain multiple variables. In recent years there has been growing popularity of multivariate designs — those involving multiple dependent variables. Two factors are primarily responsible for this trend toward more complex designs — the realization that social phenomena are complex and not easily reduced to single measures and the widespread availability of computers for data analysis.

Virtually any experimental design discussed in this monograph can be expanded to a multivariate version by collecting data on more than one dependent variable. The advantage of including multiple dependent variables in the same design is that it allows determination of complex relationships among the measures. This may be especially critical in areas where measurement is not well-developed, and the use of several different instruments may add much to the study. Multiple measures are also important in the study of complex and multidimensional phenomena. For example, task performance is not easily represented by a single variable. At the minimum performance includes elements of task speed and task accuracy. The rather basic task of typing involves typing speed, number of errors, and neatness of page layout.

The easiest way to handle multivariate data is with a series of univariate analyses, a procedure used in some of the previous univariate examples. Suppose one had data from a 2×2 factorial design with five dependent measures. One might perform a separate 2×2 ANOVA on each dependent variable and interpret each result separately. This procedure is rather simple computationally and conceptually, although interpretation could be difficult if there were differential patterns among the five variables. There is, however, one major problem with this approach and that has to do with the basic underlying probability theory upon which statistics are based. When a significance test is made, one calculates a probability that the particular findings occurred purely by chance. Normally the $p < .05$ convention is selected. For any single statistical comparison, or for all the comparisons within an ANOVA, the probability level remains at .05. However, when multiple comparisons are made with the same statistic, the probabilities do not remain at the chosen level. That is, if one were to conduct 100 comparisons at the .05 level, one would expect in the long run that 5 would be significant by chance alone. With the 2×2 design the probability of finding one or more significant effects across the five dependent variables is greater than the probability level set.

There are two ways to circumvent the probability problem with multivariate data. One could set the significance level for each comparison at a more stringent level so that overall the probability level would remain at .05. Unfortunately, this procedure is too conservative, especially with several dependent variables. If one set the level at .01, one would be forced to conclude that no significant differences were found, even if every dependent variable for every effect was significant at .02.

A better approach would be to use multivariate statistical procedures which analyze all dependent variables simultaneously. These procedures also have the advantage that they can uncover complex relationships among the dependent variables which are ignored by univariate approaches.

Most of the designs discussed in this monograph make use of ANOVA, and every one of them has a counterpart in the multivariate analysis of variance (MANOVA). Although it is more complex and requires somewhat different computational procedures, MANOVA results in a multivariate test for each effect in the design. This multivariate test indicates whether there is a significant effect for all dependent variables simultaneously. If there is an effect, additional analyses are conducted to ascertain which individual dependent variables are responsible for it and how the dependent variables are interrelated. Such analyses can become quite complex and necessitate use of computers. (For a nonmathematical introduction to MANOVA, see Spector, 1977. Tatsuoka's, 1975, monograph is a good introduction to the computational details.)

Although multivariate procedures offer a powerful way of analyzing complex data, they require considerable proficiency to utilize properly. Their use necessitates knowledge of statistical computer packages as well as the statistical procedures themselves. Their results are also considerably more difficult to interpret, and in some areas there are no clear-cut rules for interpretation. For many social scientists, use of multivariate designs would require assistance from individuals knowledgeable about multivariate methods and computers.

Examples

Factorial Design. A study by Mossholder (1980) is especially instructive because he used a 2 × 2 design with multiple dependent variables and a concomitant variable. This laboratory study was an attempt to investigate the interactive effects on intrinsic motivation of initial task interest and goal setting. Mossholder's hypothesis was that subjects who worked on an interesting task would show more intrinsic motivation when performing without a goal than with a goal, and with a boring task, intrinsic motivation would be higher for subjects with goals than without goals. The two tasks chosen, one boring and one interesting, involved putting together erector set pieces. Subjects worked under goal or no-goal conditions created by the experimenter. Three dependent variables were chosen: persistence, defined as amount of time the subject continued working on the task after the task period was concluded, task interest, and task satisfaction, each measured with two questionnaire items.

The results for each of the dependent measures are illustrated in Figure 6.4. A separate ANOVA was conducted for each dependent variable, and all three found a similar pattern of results. The interaction of goal and task was significant for all but task satisfaction which was marginal ($p < .07$), and all three main effects for task were significant.

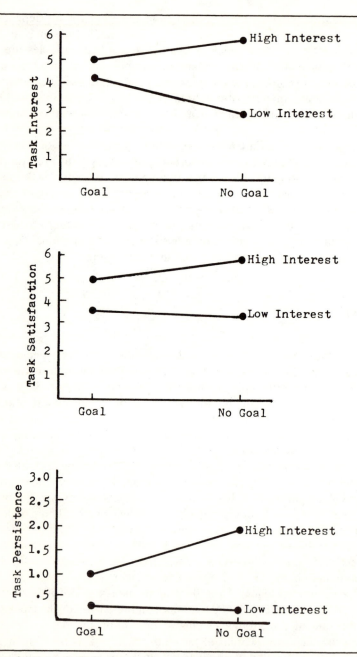

Figure 6.4   Intrinsic Motivation as a Function of Task Interest and Goals

These results can be seen in the figure, as all three graphs show the same pattern.

For additional precision, the investigator included a measure of finger dexterity as a concomitant variable. A comparison of the four treatment groups verified that there were no differences among the groups on dexterity. Thus the random assignment was successful in producing equivalent groups on at least this one important variable. However, Mossholder decided to conduct some additional analyses including finger dexterity as a covariate. He calculated an ANCOVA for each dependent variable, covarying on dexterity. He found no differences between the ANOVA and ANCOVA results.

Finally, a MANOVA was conducted on all three dependent variables simultaneously. In actuality this analysis would be conducted first, and if no differences were found for each effect, the ANOVA's would not be computed. The MANOVA's results were consistent with the ANOVA's in that the interaction was found to be significant. Mossholder failed to report the main effects which may or may not have been significant. However, his interest was only in the interaction.

Mossholder's study illustrates several points and represents the modern trend toward more complex designs and analyses. First, Mossholder recognized that intrinsic motivation can be measured several ways, so he included three measures. Of course, he might have done analyses to determine the interrelationships among these measures and whether they measured the same or different underlying variables. This would have required correlation and perhaps discriminant analysis (Spector, 1977).

Second, the use of the covariate in an attempt to increase precision was a good effort to reduce error variance in the analysis. In this particular instance, the randomization procedure was effective, and the dexterity measure did not increase sensitivity of the analyses.

This study involved a several step procedure of MANOVA, ANOVA, and ANCOVA, again showing the trend toward complexity and the use of statistical procedures in a series where the results of one analysis lead into another. Studies often involve long sequences of analyses which may check for effectiveness of independent variable manipulations, efficacy of controls, existence of confounding variables, and finally the hypotheses of interest. While such studies are complex, they can provide strong and convincing evidence for the verification or refutation of hypothesis and theory.

Higher Level Factorial Design. The higher order factorial design presented here is a 2 × 2 × 2 published by Perry, Abrami, Leventhal, and Check (1979). This study was an attempt to explore instructor-related factors that affect student evaluations of faculty. Three independent variables were manipulated: course content (high vs. low), instructor expressiveness (expressive vs. nonexpressive), and instructor reputation (positive vs. negative). The effects of these variables on overall student ratings was the focus of the study.

This study was conducted in the laboratory which allowed far greater control than would have been possible in the field. Content was manipulated by preparing the high-content lectures from actual class notes and then eliminating material for the low-content condition. Expressiveness was created by the lecturer changing style according to carefully defined roles. In the expressive condition the lecturer injected humor, physical movement, and enthusiasm into the presentation. These were excluded from the nonexpressive condition. The reputation of the instructor was manipulated by presenting subjects with either a positive or negative description of him. A series of videotaped lectures was prepared and presented to groups of students who were placed at random into one of the eight treatment groups.

The results of this study are summarized in Figure 6.5. Since this was a three-level design, two graphs were necessary to present the results. ANOVA was conducted and found significant interactions for reputation by expressiveness (Figure 6.5d) and expressiveness by content (Figure 6.5c), as well as significant main effects for reputation, expressiveness, and content.

The main effects indicated that instructors got better ratings overall if they were expressive, had positive reputations, and had high course content. The two interactions qualified these conclusions somewhat; that is, reputation affected ratings only for expressive instructors, and content was only a significant factor for nonexpressive instructors. Thus the interactions were more precise in their conclusions. It would be a mistake to conclude that content alone or reputation alone affected ratings when it was shown that they do so only under certain levels of expressiveness.

Perhaps the biggest limitation to this study is generalizability. That is, the laboratory results might not generalize to real college courses outside of the laboratory. It might well be that the subjects' knowledge of the experimental nature of the situation affected their ratings in an artificial way. However, this study indicated variables that might be critical in student ratings and suggested variables for further study in the field. In other words this study had reasonable internal validity; its external validity to field settings must be demonstrated with further research.

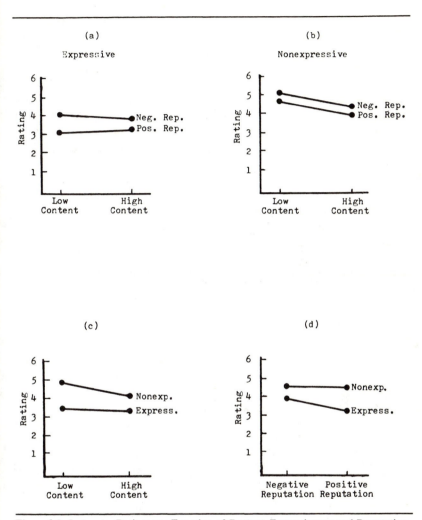

Figure 6.5 Instructor Ratings as a Function of Content, Expressiveness and Reputation

7.0 CONCLUDING REMARKS

This monograph has covered considerable material and has presented the major aspects of experimental and nonexperimental design. The reader who has understood this material now has a basic understanding of design and has at his or her fingertips many specific designs applicable to a myriad of research situations. The nonexperimental designs are extremely useful for field studies and program evaluations. Although they are often less than conclusive, they can provide much useful information which may be far superior to intuitive judgment. Furthermore, one should not overlook the value of systematic observation and assume that significant knowledge can only be gained with experimental designs. However, experimental designs are powerful tools for determining the affects that conditions or treatments have on specific behavior. Of course the astute researcher and student of design is aware of the limitations and pitfalls of even the most sophisticated experimental designs.

Design is an essential study for both the producer and consumer of research in the social sciences. Past trends that will undoubtedly continue have been toward greater sophistication in social science research methodology and the use of complex designs. The aspiring researcher would do well to consider this text as the beginning to a continuing study of design. Ancillary to that study should be a thorough treatment of statistical methods, which are essential in the analysis and interpretation of data generated by designs. There are far too many poorly designed studies that waste time, resources, and journal space, but it is difficult indeed to conduct good research or fully understand it without a strong background in design.

REFERENCES

ASHER, H. B. (1976) Causal Modeling. Beverly Hills, CA: Sage.

CAMPBELL, D. T. and J. C. STANLEY (1963) Experimental and Quasi-Experimental Designs for Research. Skokie, IL: Rand McNally.

CARMINES, E. G. and R. A. ZELLER (1979) "Reliability and Validity Assessment." Sage University Paper series on Quantitative Applications in the Social Sciences, 07-017. Beverly Hills, CA. Sage.

CHAPIN, F. S. (1955) Experimental Designs in Sociological Research. New York: Harper & Row. Cited in D. T. Campbell and J. C. Stanley (1963) Experimental and Quasi-Experimental Designs for Research. Skokie, IL: Rand McNally.

CHATFIELD, C. (1975) The Analysis of Time Series: Theory and Practice. New York: Wiley.

CHUBB, J. E. (1978) "Multiple indicators and measurement error in panel data: An evaluation of summated scales, path analysis, and confirmatory maximum liklihood factor analysis." Political Methodology 5: 413-444.

COHEN, J. and P. COHEN (1975) Applied Multiple Regression/Correlation Analysis for the Behavioral Sciences. New York: Wiley.

COLE, J. W. L. and J. E. GRIZZLE (1966) "Applications of multivariate analysis of variance to repeated measurements experiments." Biometrics 22: 810-828.

COOK, T. D. and D. T. CAMPBELL (1979) Quasi-Experimentation: Design & Analysis Issues for Field Settings. Skokie, IL: Rand McNally.

CRONBACH, L.J. and L. FURBY (1970) "How we should measure 'change' — or should we?" Psychological Bulletin 74: 68-80.

FELDT, L. S. (1958) "A comparison of the precision of three experimental designs employing a concomitant variable." Psychometrika 23: 335-353.

FREDERIKSEN, L. W. (1978) "Behavioral reorganization of a professional service system." Journal of Organizational Behavior Management 2: 1-9.

GLASS, G. V., V. L. WILLSON, and J. M. GOTTMAN (1975) Design and Analysis of Time-series Experiments. Boulder, CO: Associated University Press.

GUILFORD, J. P. (1954) Psychometric Methods. New York: McGraw-Hill.

HARRIS, C. W. [ed.] (1963) Problems in Measuring Change. Madison: University of Wisconsin Press.

IVERSEN, G. R. and H. NORPOTH (1976) "Analysis of Variance." Sage University Paper series on Quantitative Applications in the Social Sciences, 07-001. Beverly Hills, CA: Sage.

KENNY, D. A. and J. M. HARACKIEWICZ (1979) "Cross-lagged panel correlation: Practice and promise." Journal of Applied Psychology 64: 372-379.

KERLINGER, F. N. and E. J. PEDHAZUR (1973) Multiple Regression in Behavioral Research. New York: Holt, Rinehart — Winston.

KIM, J. and C. W. MUELLER (1978) "Introduction to Factor Analysis." Sage University Paper series on Quantitative Applications in the Social Sciences, 07-013. Beverly Hills, CA: Sage.

LANGBEIN, L. I. and A. J. LICHTMAN (1978) "Ecological Inference." Sage University Paper series on Quantitative Applications in the Social Sciences, 07-010. Beverly Hills, CA: Sage.

LEWIS-BECK, M. S. (1980) "Applied Regression: An Introduction." Sage University Paper series on Quantitative Applications in the Social Sciences, 07-022. Beverly Hills, CA: Sage.

MAZUR-HART, S. F. and J. J. BERMAN (1977) "Changing from fault to no-fault divorce: An interrupted time series analysis." Journal of Applied Social Psychology 7: 300-312.

McDOWALL, D., R. McCLEARY, E. E. MEIDINGER, and R. A. HAY, Jr. (1980) "Interrupted Time Series Analysis." Sage University Paper series on Quantitative Applications in the Social Sciences, 07-021. Beverly Hills, CA: Sage.

MOSSHOLDER, K. W. (1980) "Effects of externally mediated goal setting on intrinsic motivation: A laboratory experiment." Journal of Applied Psychology 65: 202-210.

MYERS, J. L. (1972) Fundamental of Experimental Design. Boston: Allyn — Bacon.

O'MALLEY, P. (1975) "Suicide and war: A case study and theoretical appraisal." British Journal of Criminology 15: 348-359.

PERRY, R. P., P. C. ABRAMI, L. LEVENTHAL, and J. CHECK (1979) "Instructor reputation: An expectancy relationship involving student ratings and achievement." Journal of Educational Psychology 71: 776-787.

POOR, D. D. S. (1973) "Analysis of variance for repeated measures designs: Two approaches." Psychological Bulletin 80: 204-209.

REILLY, R. R., M. L. TENOPYR, and S. M. SPERLING (1979) "Effects of job previews on job acceptance and survival of telephone operator candidates." Journal of Applied Psychology 64: 218-220.

ROETHLISBERGER, F. J. and M. J. DICKSON (1939) Management and the Worker. Cambridge, MA: Harvard University Press.

RUMMEL, R.J. (1970) Applied Factor Analysis. Evanston, IL: Northwestern University Press.

SPECTOR, P. E. (1980) "Techniques for handling nonorthogonal analysis of variance: A review." Evaluation Review 4: 843-855.

——— (1977) "What to do with significant multivariate effects in MANOVA." Journal of Applied Psychology 62: 158-163.

——— N. H. VOISSEM, and W. L. CONE (forthcoming) "A monte carlo study of three approaches to nonorthogonal analysis of variance." Journal of Applied Psychology.

STEPHENS, T. A. and W. A. BURROUGHS (1978) "An application of operant conditioning to absenteeism in a hospital setting." Journal of Applied Psychology 63: 518-521.

SWAMINATHAN, H. and J. ALGINA (1977) "Analysis of quasi-experimental time-series designs." Multivariate Behavioral Research 12: 111-131.

TATSUOKA, M. M. (1975) The General Linear Model: A "New" Trend in Analysis of Variance. Champaign, IL: Institute for Personality and Ability Testing.

TORGERSON, W. S. (1958) Theory and Methods of Scaling. New York: Wiley.

WALDO, G. P. and T. G. CHIRICOS (1977) "Work release and recidivism: An empirical evaluation of a social policy." Evaluation Quarterly 1: 87-108.

WILDT, A. R. and O. AHTOLA (1978) "Analysis of Covariance." Sage University Paper series on Quantitative Applications in the Social Sciences, 07-012. Beverly Hills, CA: Sage.

WINER, B.J. (1971) Statistical Principles in Experimental Design. New York: McGraw-Hill.

PAUL E. SPECTOR is currently Research Associate at the Florida Mental Health Institute in Tampa and holds a faculty appointment at the University of South Florida. He has taught both psychology and business administration and has been a mental health center program evaluator. Dr. Spector has published in the areas of statistics, psychological measurement, organizational psychology, social psychology, and program evaluation. He received his Ph.D. in industrial/organizational psychology from the University of South Florida.

Quantitative Applications
in the Social Sciences

A SAGE UNIVERSITY PAPER SERIES

$4.00 each

SAGE PUBLICATIONS, INC.
P.O. BOX 5024
BEVERLY HILLS, CALIFORNIA 90210-0024

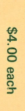

Place
Stamp
here

DATE DUE